Porch Talk

Stories of Decency, Common Sense, and Other Endangered Species

Philip Gulley

HARPER LUXE

An Imprint of HarperCollinsPublishers

HarperCollins books may be purchased for educational, business, or sales promotional use. For information please write: Special Markets Department, HarperCollins Publishers, 10 East 53rd Street, New York, NY 10022.

FIRST HARPERLUXE EDITION

HarperLuxe™ is a trademark of HarperCollins Publishers.

Library of Congress Cataloging-in-Publication Data is available upon request.

ISBN: 978-0-06-134023-9
ISBN-10: 0-06-134023-5

07 08 09 10 11 RRD (H) 10 9 8 7 6 5 4 3 2

Contents

Porch Talk

Several years back, I was visiting an elderly woman in my Quaker meeting. She was reminiscing about her childhood. I asked her what she missed the most. She closed her eyes for a moment, thinking back, then said, "Porch talk. I miss the porch talk."

Social scientists and preachers offer a number of reasons for the decline of civil society: broken homes, poverty, disease, television, and increasing secularism, to name a few. I believe all that is wrong with our world can be attributed to the shortage of front porches and the talks we had on them. Somewhere around 1950, builders left off the front porch to save money, and we've had nothing but problems ever since.

I place the blame squarely at the feet of William and Alfred Levitt, who built the first modern subdivision of

17,477 homes in a Long Island potato field in 1947. The Levitt brothers have since passed away and can't argue back. I often blame dead people for that very reason.

Prior to the subdivision, whenever people built a home, they had the good sense to add a porch. Then the Levitts thought money could be saved by not adding porches. I'm as much for saving money as the next guy, but porches are not the place to do it.

All manner of lessons were learned on the front porch. When the porches went, so did the stories and the wisdom with them. Today, we do our talking during the commercial breaks. This is a profound tragedy, but one we could correct by putting our televisions in the closet and porches on our homes.

The first years of my life, I lived in a house without a porch, in the first subdivision in our small town. When I turned nine, a grand old house with a porch came on the market. The Hollowell house. The Hollowells had been gone ten years, but the current owners hadn't resided in the house long enough for their name to adhere.

My parents would drive by it, slowing as they passed.

"Wouldn't it be wonderful to live there?" they would say to one another.

Then one Saturday morning, while Dad was walking on the town square, the owner of the jewelry store, who was also the town's realtor, stopped him.

"I have just the house for you," he told my father. "The Hollowell place. They're asking thirty thousand."

"Can't afford it," my father said.

"I can get you in that house for a thousand-dollar down payment," the jeweler-realtor said.

"I don't have a thousand dollars," my father told him.

"Write me a check, and I won't cash it until you have the money," the realtor promised.

So my father did, then and there, without telling my mother.

A few days later, the president of the bank, Hursel Disney, phoned to ask my father why he would write a check for a thousand dollars when he only had three dollars in his account.

"The realtor told me he wouldn't cash it," my father explained.

"Yeah, that's what he tells everyone," Hursel said. "Tell you what, the check just fell off my desk and landed in back of the trash can. I probably won't find it until next month."

That's the way the presidents of small-town banks did things back in those days.

And that's how we came to live in a house with a porch.

My memory is this: Each April, on the first warm Saturday, we would remove the storm windows, haul them up to the attic, carry down the screens, and fit them in the windows. The windows and screens, being old and handmade, lacked the exactness of factory windows. Someone, Mr. Hollowell, I presume, had written on each screen, in shaky, old-man handwriting, which window it fit. *Dining room, south. Northwest bedroom, window over register.* The screens never fit precisely. My father would rub a bar of soap along the frames and finesse the screens into place.

With the screens installed, we would carry the stepladder around to the front porch, lower the porch swing to its correct height, to the link in the chain with the dab of red paint, then carry the rocker up from the basement. Thus, porch season commenced.

There was an etiquette to porch sitting. People would approach our porch and stop at the foot of the steps, awaiting an invitation to join us. If one wasn't forthcoming, they knew delicate matters were being discussed and would excuse themselves after a brief exchange of pleasantries. This rule was never discussed or written down, but was generally known and obeyed by all, except by children and dull-witted adults.

Porch sitting was an evening pursuit, after the supper dishes were washed and the kitchen cleaned. We children would run underneath the streetlight, shrieking, our hands covering our hair to keep the bats out. Bats, tradition had it, made nests in your hair and drove you mad. My mother and father would watch from the porch, unconcerned, as the bats swooped past, plucking at our heads.

After a while, my mother would call us into the yard, then a while later onto the porch. Coming in for the night was always a progression. Street, yard, porch. By the time we reached the porch, we were fading and would arrange ourselves on the railing, our backs to the columns, while the adults visited. If we sat quietly and listened closely, we could hear them discuss matters we weren't ordinarily privy to, stories of certain people in our town who'd moved away without telling anyone.

Some evenings, if my father was feeling expansive, he would share stories of his childhood, about growing up in what he called the "hard times." In later conversations with my Aunt Doris, I learned many of my father's stories were embellished, which in no way lessened their appeal.

On nights the Cincinnati Reds played, my father would set the kitchen radio on the parlor table, open the window onto the porch, and listen to Marty Brennaman announce the game. Lee Comer would wander over from next door to provide local commentary. Lee was exempt from the rules of porch etiquette. He and any member of his family could ascend the steps without asking, and still can, since Lee's son, Ben, now owns the house, even though it's still called the Gulley house.

Porch talk is one of the customs we've let slide out of our lives, not realizing how desperately it is needed. We're like Mark Nickerson, a child who lived two houses down from us and ate chalk. When I asked my mother why, she told me his body probably lacked some important nutrient, which caused him to crave chalk. There is a house on the edge of our town that cost an obscene amount. Its porch is a tiny footprint of cement. A week after the new family moved in, a chair appeared outside the door, crowded among the landscaping. It's the Mark Nickerson phenomena. The family craved a porch; they just didn't know it. We were better off when porches were standard equipment.

This is the irony—we have more talk than ever before, but too little communication; so many words, but so little meaning. "Bombardment" is the word that comes to mind—talk radio, twenty-four-hour news, hundreds of television channels, and, God help us all, gas pumps that spout the news along with fuel—coarse exchanges fraying the ties that bind.

I miss those days of lag time, of sitting on the porch swing with my grandmother, when large chunks of summer days would pass with scarcely a word between us, her fingers caressing a rosary, me whittling a stick, the silence full and rich and comfortable. My grandmother was not long on advice, but something she told me, when my interest in romance was on the rise, remains with me still. "Philip, be sure to marry someone you can be silent with and not be anxious." So I did, while also gravitating toward a religion, Quakerism, that esteemed companionable silence.

The magic of our porch talks, I now recall, was not only their depth, but their breadth. My grandmother supplied the depth, and I provided the scattering of topics, a hint of my future as a commentator on matters large and small. We discussed Lawrence Welk, the Virgin Mary, Richard Nixon, the gold standard, and the merits of homemade ice cream versus store-bought. I especially remember a fascinating talk about my family's history with moonshine.

I do not wish to romanticize the porch. Not all of its talk reached the level of Plato or Jefferson, but there was a luster to those talks, a certain glow and depth lacking in these days of e-mail and instant messaging. Perhaps it was the parenthesis of silence, the bracketing of conversation with reflection.

When my wife and I bought our home, we gave careful consideration to the number of bedrooms and bathrooms. Little did we realize the most valuable real estate would be the two hundred square feet of our porch. On it, we have solved all of the world's problems, evening after pleasant evening, arcing back and forth in our wicker swing, the twilight breeze bearing all our cares away.

A Curious Obsession

At last count, we owned sixty-four chairs. I'm not certain how we ended up with so many, but after twenty-two years of marriage, that's where we stand. When my son Sam was in first grade, his teacher asked the children to go home that evening and count the chairs in their home. Sam buried his head in his hands and moaned, "No, not the chairs. Please, not the chairs."

Several years ago, on a visit to the doctor, I was reading a magazine and saw a picture of a man sitting in what was described as the world's most comfortable rocking chair. Through dogged detective work, I tracked down the man who'd made it to a small town in Texas and asked if he would make one for me. Naturally, before ordering it, I sought my wife's consent. In fact, I asked her that very evening. Actually, it was early the next day, around two o'clock in the morning, though now she says she doesn't remember.

When I talked with the man in Texas, he asked what I did. I told him I was a Quaker pastor. I didn't tell him I was a writer. He would have asked the names of the books I've written, I'd have told him, and he'd have said, in the typically blunt manner old men have, "Never heard of them." Who needs the humiliation?

Like most people who meet ministers, he felt obligated to report on his ecclesial standing. "I'm not a regular churchgoer," he said.

"What kind of church do you avoid attending?" I asked him.

"Southern Baptist," he said. "I guess my religion is making chairs."

Chairs are a religion I understand.

Years ago, I made a rocker. I didn't have a plan or blueprint; I just had the idea of a chair in my mind and went from there. The first time I sat in it, it rocked back too far and dumped me on the ground. I gave it to my brother-in-law.

My favorite chair is one my grandfather gave me. It is nearly two hundred years old. He rescued it from a priest who was getting ready to throw it on a burn pile. The average priest knows nothing about chairs.

I once owned a rocker made around 1875 by the Shakers of Mt. Lebanon, Massachusetts. The Shakers who made the chairs never signed them, fearing it would appear boastful. I wasn't nearly as modest. When I made my chair, I signed it, hoping someday it would serve as proof of my existence.

There is a certain transcendent joy in creating a thing of beauty. But even more fulfilling is to become a being of beauty.

I contemplate the difference between *thing* and *being*—how often we confuse the two, reducing others to what they do, calculating their importance by what they own, not who they are. "He's worth a fortune," we say of the rich man, as if wealth confers worth. The most beautiful soul I ever knew died penniless, sweet confirmation that although possessions might ease life, they don't ennoble it.

A prosperous man turned poet, Harindranath Chattopadhyaya once wrote:

In early days I used to be
A poet through whose pen
Innumerable songs would come
To win the hearts of men;
But now, through new-got knowledge
Which I hadn't had so long,

I have ceased to be the poet
And have learned to be the song.

The man from Texas signs his chairs. But when the ink fades, so will his legacy. This is true for all of us. Which is why we should cease to be the poet and learn to be the song.

Charley

The demise of the independent hardware store will surely rank as one of the greatest tragedies in American history. After years of scientific research, I have observed a correlation between the decline of hardware stores and the rise of depression. When Baker's Hardware Store in my hometown closed in 1988, it plunged hundreds of men into a sadness from which we've still not recovered. We talk about it on Saturday mornings at the Courthouse Grounds. "Boy, I sure wish Baker's hadn't closed," I say. The men around the table stir their coffee; a veil of sorrow descends over the coffee shop. They all agree it was a crying shame.

A new hardware store has opened in our town, but we are not sure whether it is a hardware flirtation or a true marriage, so we're holding back to see if it endures.

Businesses have a way of springing up like flowers in our town, only to fade in the heat of day. It's best not to get one's hopes up.

There is, in Roachdale, Indiana, a hardware store of unparalleled excellence. The owner is Charley Riggle, a fitting name for a hardware man. Every good hardware man I've ever known was named Charley or Leonard or Hank. Charley is walking sunshine and a balm to the spirits. A stream of men move through his store at any given time, walking the aisles, studying the merchandise. One gets the impression they aren't looking for anything to buy, so much as needing an excuse to spend time in such an agreeable place. It is a town of hard workers where loafing is frowned upon and must be disguised as a trip to the hardware store.

Roachdale Hardware began life as Bowen Hardware in 1900. It has wood floors and a working 1949 Coke machine from which you can buy a bottle of pop for a dime. Due to the ravages of inflation, you also have to put seventy-five cents in a plastic bowl on top of the Coke machine.

On my first visit to Roachdale Hardware, I spied a Case jigged-bone Autumn Blaze Baby Butterbean pocketknife and bought it. I had gone knifeless for thirty-three years, and the weight of it in my pocket was a pleasure. I carry my pocketknife with me at all times and have been in a better mood ever since. The experience of buying the knife—of studying the various knives in their clean rows, hefting each one, testing its weight and balance—was so satisfying, I've bought twenty-one Case pocketknives since. I still haven't figured out whether I return to the Roachdale hardware store for the knives or for Charley.

Charley keeps the knives in a case up front near the door, in between the screwdrivers and the snow shovels.

"That there's a 1950 display case," Charley told me, with no small amount of pride. Charley has lots of old things in his store and knows the precise age of each one.

People say happiness can't be found in possessions. That depends on the possession. Having a new pocketknife can boost a man's spirits like nothing else. A man with a knife in his pocket is only a memory away from his youth, of whittling under a shade tree on a summer day, of playing mumblety-peg at recess back when boys carried knives to school, of carving his sweetheart's name in a beech tree.

Roachdale Hardware holds other fascinations—a 1906 Rain or Shine buggy in the front window, an antique rolling ladder Charley climbs to reach the air filters, and an 1890 safe from the Cary Safe Company of Buffalo, New York. The combination was written on a piece of paper that Charley lost, so now he stores his office supplies in the safe. These various ingredients, though singly unimpressive, combine to form a pleasant stew.

Charley is the whole show at Roachdale Hardware. When he and his wife go to Michigan for a week every summer, the place closes down. The prudent customer anticipates Charley's absence and schedules his household emergencies for when the hardware store is open.

I never visit Charley unless I have sufficient time to sit on the bench back by the cash register, drink a Coke, view the latest pictures of his granddaughter, and talk about pocketknives. Men wander in and out of the store, some adding to the coffers, others not, seeking Charley's counsel on a plumbing or electrical matter.

I have met some hardware storeowners who lack diplomacy, who blab stories of home maintenance mishaps all over town. Charley is the picture of discretion, as tight-lipped as a priest after confession. Once while I was there, a man returned three times in the span of an hour, a tragic figure, cursed by a home repair project that had gone south.

"What's his problem?" I asked Charley after he'd left.

Charley pretended he hadn't heard me and deftly changed the subject. My admiration for him soared.

There is a moral sturdiness to Charley that isn't advertised or boasted about, but is obvious to all who know him and quickly discerned by those who don't. Our country has lately been afflicted with television preachers and pundits who focus on our families while neglecting theirs. How vainglorious these critics seem, how vacuous and shallow they appear when placed alongside a man of Charley's stature.

I cannot separate Charley from his store; one without the other would seem incomplete, like a nut without a bolt. It's their sum that is crucial. The hardware store is the community shrine and Charley its high priest with all his sacred duties—counselor, comforter, confessor, and friend. I am a congregant, one of Charley's flock. Even though I walk through the valley of the shadow of home maintenance, I fear no evil, for Charley is with me; his advice and unflappability, they comfort me.

Home Depot would pay millions to replicate the native wisdom and goodwill one finds at Roachdale Hardware or any other small-town hardware store that dots our land. This is why we men at the Courthouse Grounds still grieve the death of Baker's Hardware these many years later. We know what we have lost and it wasn't just a store; it was our sanctuary. Some of us went there to preach, others to listen, some to heal, others to be healed. Our sins were confessed in her dim corners, our hymns of thanksgiving sung in her aisles. Now it is gone, and we are pilgrims, wandering in the wilderness, seeking our promised land, the fading memory of hardware fellowship spurring us on.

The Jig's Up

As a pastor, I hear my share of hard-luck stories, but a recent conversation with the Tooth Fairy topped them all.

"It's tough out there," she told me. "Kids used to be happy to get a nickel. Now all I hear is griping." Her wings were tattered, her skirt patched. "I don't know how much longer I can go on like this. I might have to file for bankruptcy."

"It's simple mathematics," she told me. "When I started in this business, there were a couple hundred people and money hadn't been invented. I used to put pebbles under the children's pillows and they were happy with that. Now there's nearly seven billion people and the kids all want a dollar."

I'm doing my part. My youngest child's last baby tooth just fell out, so we're no longer on the dole.

There is something about a child's last tooth, hanging on by a scrap of gum and nerve, that pains a parent's heart. This is it. No more baby teeth. No more sneaking in at night and nudging their head aside to slip a coin under their pillow. No more baby teeth to add to the stockpile I keep hidden in my underwear drawer. At first glance, the teeth appear as tiny white pieces of gravel. On closer look, you can make out dried blood in the crevasses, then the smoothed point of a root. Teeth.

I used to separate them, Spencer's teeth from Sam's, but while I wasn't watching, the teeth integrated, humanity seeking humanity in the chaotic debris of my top dresser drawer. Now they're lumped together in a plastic sandwich bag, which our son, Sam, found while rifling through my chest of drawers in search of treasure.

He's a bright boy, our Sam, and quickly put two and two together.

"Is there a Tooth Fairy?" he asked me.

"Yes," I told him, not mentioning our role in the enterprise.

"Then why do you have the teeth?"

I pointed out that, although one tooth weighed hardly anything, millions of teeth are lost each day, burdening even the most stalwart fairy, so the teeth are entrusted to the parents.

This satisfied him for a day. The next afternoon, he called me back to the witness stand. He cut to the chase. "You're the Tooth Fairy, aren't you?"

"Yes."

He stared at me, warily. "What about Santa Claus?"

"What about him?"

"Is that you too?"

"Yes, your mother and I."

"The Easter Bunny?"

I nodded my head.

"Jesus?"

"Oh, no. He's real."

But I could tell Sam had his doubts.

I talk with the Tooth Fairy because conversations with my children have become too complex.

I have lost credibility with my children, having been branded a teller of tales.

Now the day has arrived for The Talk. The Big One. The Birds and the Bees One. And they won't believe a word I say.

My wife predicted this would happen when I persisted with the myth of Santa Claus in the face of their initial doubts. "They won't trust you," she warned. "Then one day you'll need them to believe you, and they won't."

Which means she has to be the one to tell them about sex.

Gee, I hate that.

Call Me Coach

I have a friend who, like me, is a Quaker pastor, though he pursues the vocation with more passion. His office bookshelves are lined with how-to-pastor books. We meet for lunch occasionally. He talks about the books he's read, and I nod my head and smile, feigning acquaintance with the texts, then eat my sandwich.

Not long ago, our lunchtime conversation took a curious turn.

"I had lunch with my coach yesterday," he said.

For as long as I've known him, my friend has been a klutz, so I was surprised to hear he had a coach. Then it occurred to me he was probably speaking about the coach of his church's softball team.

"Are you fielding a good team this year?" I asked. He'd been known to sneak a ringer or two on the team.

We Quakers lack a fighting spirit and have to draft a few Baptists to add vigor to the roster.

"What are you talking about?" he asked.

"You mentioned your softball coach, so I asked if you had a good team this year."

"Not my softball coach," he said. "My life coach."

"Your life coach? What's a life coach?"

My friend rolled his eyes. He often does that when we're together. "My life coach helps me maximize my potential. He enhances my life performance."

"Plain English please," I said.

"He tells me what to do."

"And you pay him to do this?"

"Yes, and he's not cheap. One hundred dollars a session."

No Quaker minister I've ever met could afford a life coach, but my friend's wife had recently inherited some money, and he was frittering it away in a vain effort to maximize his potential and enhance his life performance. If my wife ever hit the jackpot, the last thing I'd do is pay someone to tell me what to do. I'd spend it on really important things, like a new motorcycle and power tools and pocketknives.

I told my friend I would be his life coach for fifty dollars a session.

He asked if I was a certified life coach.

"Better than that. I come from a long line of coaches. It's in my blood."

For as long as I can remember, my mother has been training me to be a life coach. I realize that now, though I was unacquainted with that term until recently. But that's what she's been doing, mostly by setting an example.

"Do you want to know what I think?" she would ask me, when I was a child. Then she would proceed to tell me, without waiting to hear my answer. That is a mother's prerogative and I never resented it, though I thought it would abate when I flew the coop. But she's still at it, coaching me at every turn, and I'm doing all I can to carry that legacy forward.

I pass out advice like candy at a parade, tossing it out indiscriminately to whoever will receive it. Every Sunday morning I tell my congregation what to do. I'm not like those pastors on television who bluster and scold and lack subtlety. I'm sneaky about it. I try to make it appear as if the advice I'm offering was something I learned from them. That's an old life-coach trick—*make folks think it was their idea!*

I've not limited my coaching to people in my church. I also tell members of my family what to do. I once gave my aunt a hot tip on a stock. When she lost two thousand dollars, it provided her a handsome tax write-off, for which she seemed profoundly grateful. "I don't know how I can thank you," she told me several times. In fact, I've given her so many tips over the years, she no longer even pays taxes. Indeed, her financial situation has been altered so significantly the government now gives her money *and free cheese*. This is the kind of synergy we life coaches strive for.

I began my career as a life coach when I was a teenager and advised my friend Bill Eddy to ride his bicycle down a hill as fast as he could with his eyes closed and his hands behind his back. Oddly enough, he wrecked and was taken to the hospital with several broken bones. Fortunately, his stay in the hospital helped him overcome his fear of doctors. I'm pleased I had a hand in his learning to trust others.

When I know someone might be hard up, I don't even charge to coach that person. A few months ago, I installed a set of gas logs in a friend's fireplace. I think he did something wrong, because when he lit the logs, a fireball erupted, scorching his hair and knocking him across the room. It's a good thing I was present and able to phone the fire department, who arrived in time to save nearly half his home. I shudder to think how bad it might have been if I hadn't been there to help him.

Occasionally, I have been accused of sticking my nose in where it doesn't belong, but life coaches often go where mere mortals fear to tread. We can't let a little thing like scorn keep us from our appointed rounds.

Since I spoke to my pastor friend about hiring a life coach, I've met a number of folks who've employed them. I'm not sure how this trend developed, but suspect it has something to do with the decline of the neighborhood sage. When I was a kid, every block had at least one. It was generally an old man or woman. The man could be found in a back corner of his garage, building birdhouses or applying varnish to a wooden screen door. The woman could be found on a front porch, shelling peas or doing needlework. But they were always plentiful and willing to offer all sorts of counsel, bidden or unbidden.

Now we've been taught to fear those people, to not speak to strangers, to look for sinister motives where none exist. So we're filling this wisdom vacancy in other ways, turning to life coaches, television, therapists, movie-star preachers, and radio commentators, when the prophets are just down the street. In my childhood, it was Doc Gibbs and Mrs. Harvey, both of whom oozed sound judgment from every pore.

That wisdom hasn't gone anywhere. In a culture that prizes glitz, celebrity, and youthfulness, we've forgotten where to find it. But whenever I spend an hour with anyone over eighty I come away impressed by their level-headedness and embarrassed by my lack of it. Some of us life coaches are pale pretenders, tooting our horns, while the real teachers sit quietly in their corners, waiting for an audience that never arrives.

Pond Life

I've always wanted waterfront property, but the local geography has never cooperated, except to occasionally fill our basement with water. I tried talking my wife into buying a lakefront cabin, but she resisted. "Most of the people in the world don't own one house. Why should we own two?"

I pointed out that the same thing could be said of toothbrushes, but she didn't budge.

Eventually, it occurred to me that instead of moving my family to water, I could move the water to my family. "Let's put in a pond," I suggested to Joan. "We could fill it with fish and water lilies and have a little waterfall and listen to the gurgle of water. It would be just like living beside a mountain stream."

"Mountain stream" proved to be a winning combination of words, and Joan consented.

Within a week, three teenage boys were digging a large hole beside our patio, heaping the dirt on one end for a waterfall. I sat in a lawn chair and supervised, which was hard enough, given how teenagers resist direction. After the hole was dug, it was lined with rubber, surrounded by stacked stone, then filled with water. I plugged in the pump, a faint whoosh was heard, and water began tumbling over the stones, our own little Niagara.

"Let's get some fish," Joan said, warming to the idea of waterfront property.

We read a book about goldfish and koi and how not to kill them, then spent a tidy sum of money buying a dozen fish to stock our pond. We followed the book precisely, gradually acclimating the fish to our pond, fine-tuning the pH balance to provide the optimum environment. The third morning, Sam rushed in the house to share the happy news that our fish knew how to swim on their backs. The second bunch of fish lasted nearly a week before a wandering herd of raccoons eviscerated them. The fish that replaced them died of a gruesome fungus, and the batch after that was a midnight snack for a great blue heron.

The boy next door, Johnny, shunning every rule of proper fish handling, filched a goldfish from a neighbor's pond, carried it around in his pocket for half a day, taking it out every now and then to dunk in water, and then finally, almost as an afterthought, pitched it in our pond, where it has thrived, growing to immense proportions. I woke up one night to the sound of gagging and had to perform the Heimlich maneuver on a great blue heron who'd managed to get the fish lodged in its throat. The heron spat the goldfish halfway across the pond, staggered away, and hasn't been seen since.

Fish, we read in our fish book, keep a pond free of mosquitoes, but our fish is a slacker in the insect department. At the start, clouds of mosquitoes regularly rose from our pond, exposing us to a host of diseases. Fortunately, a thick scum of algae soon coated the pond, choking out the mosquitoes. The algae is now so dense I can walk upon the waters, startling passersby and boosting my reputation.

I have seen magazine pictures of pristine ornamental ponds surrounded by lush flora, with attractive people enjoying witty conversation in the cool shade. Those pictures were not taken at my home.

Shortly after the pond was dug, in a reckless moment, I added two tadpoles to it, hoping one of them would survive to adulthood. I wasn't aware that frogs are religious, but mine must be Roman Catholic. They have sired numerous offspring and are still going at it. Scientists maintain that frogs are declining in number, disappearing from wetlands, but I can assure you that reports of their demise are exaggerated.

Poets wax eloquent about the croak of the bullfrog and the throb of the spring peeper, but my family can't sleep for the racket. The frogs have taken over our patio—green thugs in black T-shirts, toting their skateboards, blaring their music, sneering at us as we hurry past, our eyes averted.

A man down the road stopped by the house last summer to see our pond. In junior high school, he'd bullied me mercilessly, and I've wanted to pay him back ever since.

"How do you like your pond?" he asked. "I've been thinking of putting one in."

"You won't regret it," I told him. "They're so relaxing. Plus, they increase the value of your home."

Worry lines now crease his face and large bags have formed under his eyes.

He phoned me one evening this past spring. "How do you get rid of mosquitoes?"

"Oh, that's easy. You get frogs. Start with tadpoles. But they die off easily, so you should buy several dozen."

That so much misery could emanate from such a small area is a wonder.

When our pond was first installed, a recovering pond owner asked me why I'd decided to mess up what had been a perfectly good life.

I told him I had loved a pond in my childhood.

It was a pond in the field behind our home. It had begun life as a stream. Then an ambitious neighbor with a bulldozer fashioned an earthen dam and the waters rose behind it, forming the arena for many of my childhood adventures.

In the summer of my tenth year, Wally at Logan's Mobil patched a truck inner tube and gave it to me. I lashed several boards across the top and poled the raft across the pond. In the winter, we stretched rope across each end of the pond to serve as hockey goals. When winter gave way to spring, before the bugs set in, we would camp on its shore, loosed from the tether of parental oversight. One summer, I very nearly talked a local beauty into skinny dipping with me, but at the last moment her Methodist virtue carried the day. That pond played a central role in my adolescent yearnings, the stage for travel, bedlam, freedom, and romance.

There are things—houses, fields, lakes—that loom large in our childhood and then when visited in later years are diminished. That pond was once an ocean, but now can be cleared in three steps and a hop. I have no idea where that water went, just as I have no idea how my smooth skin and hair were lost.

Like most attempts to re-create the charms of one's past, this venture into pond life has been a mixed one, the moments of transcendence few. The cast and crew who populate my speckled memories are now gone, a few of them dead, most of them dispersed across the country. But some nights, while I'm lying in bed, the frogs will commence their evening clamor, and I am thirteen again, camping with Tim Hadley at the pond, discussing matters of great import—Methodist girls, cars, Baptist girls, hunting, Quaker girls. We were nothing if not ecumenical.

Tim can no longer enjoy the pleasure of reminiscence. A drunken driver took his life in 1981. Sometimes, while sitting by my pond, I think of Tim and our pond life. I think of the wife he never married, the children he never had, and it occurs to me that, although some things (houses, fields, lakes) diminish over time, other things (loss, grief, the heartbreak of lives cut short) do not. There is much good to recollect while seated by my pond, and much sorrow too, and sometimes they are one and the same.

The Slow Life

Two or three times a week I visit the Dairy Queen in our town. When I was a child, I went for the ice cream. When a teenager, I went for the girls who worked behind the counter. Now I go to visit Leon, who owns the Dairy Queen and presides over the enterprise from a lawn chair at the back door. He has much time to think, and I like to stop by there and rummage among his musings. We were recently discussing the peculiarities of modern life, when he said, "We're so busy living the good life, we've forgotten how to enjoy life."

Not everything Leon says sticks in my mind, but that observation has. There is not an ounce of hypocrisy in Leon. He not only extols the merits of relaxation; he embodies it. I don't know anyone who sits as well as he does—hour after hour, moving from nap to conversation to nap again, every now and then reaching down to scratch his dog behind its ears. If leisure were an Olympic sport, Leon would be a gold medalist.

Leon is not lazy. For many years, he worked two jobs; he was an accountant in the daytime and king of the Dairy Queen evenings and weekends. Now it is his season for leisure, and he pursues it with the same single-minded determination he's shown in all his endeavors.

I find myself wishing Leon's dedication to leisure was contagious. I know people who don't take their allotted vacation from work, who willingly surrender those precious days to corporations that would boot them out the door tomorrow to save a dollar. I want to buy them a chair and place them beside Leon, in hopes his spirit of relaxation would be transmitted.

I was thinking about Leon and our affinity for busyness, when I happened upon a book called *In Praise of Slowness*, written by Carl Honoré. In that book he describes a *New Yorker* cartoon that illustrates our dilemma. Two little girls are standing at a school-bus stop, each clutching a personal planner. One says to the other, "Okay, I'll move ballet back an hour, reschedule gymnastics, and cancel piano. You shift your violin lessons to Thursday and skip soccer practice.

That gives us from 3:15 to 3:45 on Wednesday the six-teenth to play."

This, I suppose, is how the madness starts.

Pay close attention to the words Honoré uses to de-scribe this fast-life/slow-life dichotomy. "Fast is busy, controlling, aggressive, hurried, analytical, stressed, su-perficial, impatient, active, quantity-over-quality. Slow is the opposite: calm, careful, receptive, intuitive, un-hurried, patient, reflective, quality-over-quantity. . . . It is seeking to live at what musicians call the *tempo giusto*—the right speed."*

Which of those lifestyles would you prefer?

I purchased numerous copies of the book, distrib-uted them to my friends, and suggested we form a book study and meet twice a week to discuss it, but we were all too busy.

I've been wondering at the forces that propel our haste and have concluded that clocks have much to do with it. When Leon sits at the Dairy Queen, his back is turned to all timepieces and their nagging, prod-ding authority. He cannot see the clock hanging over Joe Neher's Heat and Cool shop or the clock above the

---

*From Carl Honoré, *In Praise of Slowness: Challenging the Cult of Speed* (San Francisco: HarperSanFrancisco, 2004), pp. 14–15.

garage at the Weaver-Randolph Funeral Home. Nor can he see the Dairy Queen clock. It is through the door and around the corner. His wristwatch is at home, on top of his bureau. Out of sight, out of mind, out of step, and delightedly so.

My friend Jim refuses to wear a watch; he is unwilling to let a numbered dial dictate the pace of his life. (This in no way prevents him from asking me the time whenever we're together.)

There is no escaping these scolds. They are everywhere we look—in our cars, strapped to our bodies, hanging on every wall, beside our beds, on our appliances and cell phones, and, Lord help us, with the aid of digital technology now shining forth from our bathroom mirrors. And what is their common theme? Hurry! Hurry! Hurry! You are late! There is much to do, and you are already behind!

Several years ago, a friend gave me a clock that is connected, through the ether, to an atomic clock in Colorado. It shows the precise time, to the tenths of a second. It makes me nervous just to look at it. I would throw it away, but he visits my home often, always pausing to study my clock. "My gosh," he says, "I had no idea it was that time. I must go."

Inspired by Leon's example of restorative leisure, I asked my church for a summer off. To make it sound official, I called it a sabbatical. The word "sabbatical" is derived from the word *sabbatikos,* which is Greek for "goofing off while giving the impression of earnest study." The first two months I relaxed, then during the third month I buckled down and went on vacation.

It seems odd that I would have to leave my church to restore my soul, but that is precisely what happened. A woman in my meeting was opposed to the sabbatical. "Idle hands are the devil's workshop," she warned me. I didn't find the devil in my leisure. I found mindfulness, clarity, and renewal. Sometimes those who hesitate aren't lost, but found.

One of the qualities I most admire about Jesus was his high regard for the right speed. Never one to rush panting toward some desired goal, he noticed what others overlooked—a crippled man beside the pool of Siloam, a woman at a well, a tax collector looking on from a tree. The church attributed such sensitivity to his divine nature, which conveniently excused us from being like him. But I contend, as did he, that such attentiveness, such well-paced and measured living, can also be ours. "And why are you anxious? Consider the lilies of the field, how they grow; they toil not, nor do they spin" (Matthew 6:28).

But in a world where time is money, where idle hands are the devil's workshop, those who live the slow life are seen as suspect, if not heretical. To them, I simply say that when God spoke to Elijah, it was not in the earthquake, wind, or fire, but in a small and restful voice, a divine drawl, if you will, a porch voice.

And what does that voice tell us? To not be so busy living the good life we've forgotten how to enjoy life.

You Get What
You Pay For

Several years ago, I purchased a cheap pair of shoes
in order to save twenty dollars. The shoes didn't
provide sufficient support for my feet and knees, and I
had to spend several hundred dollars on doctor's visits,
X-rays, and medicine. Joan wanted to give the shoes
to Goodwill, but I wouldn't let her. They were hardly
broken in, and I was determined to get my money's
worth from them, even if it crippled me.

I spend a great deal of money trying to save it.

Not long ago I spent thirty-five hundred dollars
to have my car painted. It was dented and dingy, but
otherwise in good condition. I had the clever idea that
painting the car would be cheaper than replacing it.
Two months after having it painted, I still had a low
opinion of the car, sold it for three thousand dollars,

and bought a new one. With my track record, I could work for the government.

Last summer, a cedar tree flanking our front door attracted a horde of bagworms, which proceeded to strip it clean and kill it. I reasoned it would take three hours to secure another tree, plant it, and dispose of the old one. Like everyone else, I have only my time to sell and estimated it would be thirty dollars cheaper to hire a nurseryman to replace the cedar than to do it myself. While he was at our house, I decided to have him do a few other things for me. When he finished a week later, I was out four thousand dollars. If I keep saving money at this rate, I'm going to soon be broke.

Not all of my financial decisions have been catastrophic. Some have been merely ruinous. When my wife and I were first married, we pinched pennies and managed to save three thousand dollars, which we used to purchase stock in a company. Five years later, we sold the stock for a modest gain and purchased a used car. You won't be surprised to learn that as soon as we sold the stock, it skyrocketed. It would now be worth well over a hundred thousand dollars. The car we'd purchased had a thirty-day warranty. The engine blew on the thirty-second day, and we had to pay a man a hundred dollars to haul it away.

I'm not the only person who spends money to save it. I have a friend who bought a riding mower because it was on sale for two hundred dollars off. But it didn't fit in his garage and he ended up buying a three-thousand-dollar utility barn to store it in. Whenever I visit, he points out his mower and how he saved two hundred dollars.

I wish I could save money like that. A little while back, I added up how much money I'd earned over the years and it came to several million dollars. I checked our savings account to see if Joan had put it there, but it was empty. Then it occurred to me that I had spent most of it at the Dairy Queen.

A few weeks later, I saw an ice cream maker at a hardware store for a hundred and seventy-eight dollars and ninety-eight cents. I remembered the millions of dollars I'd spent at the Dairy Queen and thought it was time I started making my own ice cream. So I purchased the ice cream maker, then went to the grocery store and bought the ingredients for ice cream, which cost another ten dollars. It made two quarts of ice cream, which could have been purchased at a store for four dollars. But I haven't been back to the Dairy Queen since. In fact, I haven't been anywhere since. Eating all that heavy cream aggravated my colon, and I'm having to stick close to home.

Fortunately, I've made a few good financial decisions over the years that have really paid off. When my wife and I were first married, the man who does our taxes advised us to buy stock in a company owned by some guy from Nebraska we'd never heard of—Jimmy Buffet, or something like that. We put it in the Christmas club down at the bank instead, then used the money to buy a set of mixing bowls that we're still using. It's that kind of savvy that has set my wife and me on the sound financial footing we enjoy today.

The Compact

My father, who for years never had a good word to say about taxes, was elected to be the tax assessor for our town and has lately switched his tune. He visits each new home, assesses its value, then determines the amount of property taxes its owner must pay. Before he took the job, he was a well-liked man and people were happy to see him, but now his popularity is fading.

Not long ago, I stopped by his office to visit. A woman was there complaining about her property taxes, which she thought were excessive. No one ever tells my father their taxes are too low. My father, ever the diplomat, made a joke about taxes, but the woman didn't laugh. Then he tried the taxes-help-our-town approach. "It goes to pay for schools," he explained.

"It pays for our library, and our police and firefighters. We use it to care for our parks and build sidewalks and keep the roads in good repair. We do a lot of good with the money."

She said, "I don't care about those things. I don't care about the schools. I don't have children. Why should I have to pay to educate other people's children?"

Civilized societies have long wrestled with the idea of collective responsibility, of caring for children not our own. The French philosopher Rousseau coined the term *social compact* to describe this phenomenon. Rousseau believed that for a community to thrive, its citizens had to each cede a portion of their wealth and power to the common good in exchange for certain rights and protections. If we weren't willing to do this, we would revert back to the law of the jungle, where, as Thucydides said, "The strong do as they can, while the weak suffer what they must."

When the lady paused from screeching at my father, I told her about the social compact, but she wasn't interested. It turns out a lot of people aren't interested in it, especially when they discover it isn't free.

I've devised a one-question test to demonstrate the merit of the social compact: Would you rather live in Switzerland, a country with a high regard for the social compact, or Sudan, a country whose social compact has fallen apart? I've asked that question of a dozen people, all of whom were complaining about taxes. No one has ever chosen Sudan. The problem is that we all want Switzerland without having to pay for it.

Take my money, please. I don't want it if it means my children and grandchildren will be afflicted with second-rate schools, third-world health care, shuttered libraries, busted dreams, and broken cities.

I'm not sure how or when it happened, but somewhere along the way the word "taxes" became a dirty word. No one ever has a good word to say about them. We demand they be slashed here and sliced there. More recently, we've replaced the progressive income tax—that quaint notion that Donald Trump should pay a higher percentage of his income in taxes than a single mother flipping burgers at McDonald's—with the lottery. Oh, the lottery, our modern-day shell game that preys on the poor, the helpless and hopeless, so our government can finance tax breaks for General Electric and Halliburton.

I once visited a church and gave a rousing speech on the benefits of progressive taxation. It was a well-heeled flock and not many folks bothered to shake my hand after the service. One man did pause and advise me to stick to the Bible. I'm not sure what part of the Bible he'd been reading, so I directed him to the eighth chapter of Amos. "Hear this, you who trample upon the needy and bring the poor of the land to an end. . . . I will turn your feasts into mourning and all your songs into lamentations" (vv. 4, 10).

One of the deepest pleasures in my life is quoting the Bible back to people who quote it to me.

Smooth politicians wax eloquent about their Christian faith, then vote to toss the vulnerable and desperate to the lions. Preachers in thousand-dollar suits pitch the blessings of God on cable television. Our social compact lies beaten and broken along the road, while greed and hubris strut by, unmindful and uncaring. Children cry for bread, and we give them stones. To them, our beloved, the fruit of our loins and joy of our hearts, we have bequeathed a broken infrastructure, crime borne of despair, minimum wages, and maximum misery. Not to mention the obliteration of the middle class, communal disarray, and the unchecked power of the rich. We inherited a Switzerland and are passing on a Sudan, as our children reap the bitter harvest of a splintered social compact.

Someday, I hope to vote for a politician who doesn't think "tax" is a dirty word. Almost every benefit we've ever enjoyed happened because our ancestors were generous enough to share their resources for the good of the whole. Their tax dollars educated us, secured our health, promoted our safety, and enhanced our lives immeasurably.

Shortly after my wife was born, the township she lived in voted not to pay its library tax. Then a relatively prosperous township made up of small family farms, it believed that particular tax was a waste of money. As a consequence, the children of that township were not allowed to use the public library. My wife didn't check a book out of a public library until she was twenty-one. She remembers wanting to enter and being told it was forbidden. Today, that township is one of the poorest townships in the state's second poorest county, less than ten percent of its children go to college, and they still believe they can't afford to pay their library tax.

When America thrived, it thrived because its citizenry invested heavily in one another. If America fails, it will be because we have placed our personal gain above the common good. If that day comes, a few of us might be richer, but we will all be infinitely poorer.

The Tornado

Visit on a porch long enough in my town and eventually the conversation will wind its way around to March 26, 1948, when the tornado hit. Nearly sixty years later it's still called *the* tornado. Tornados have struck our town since, but none with the single-minded determination of that Good Friday tornado. Some people remember where they were when they learned of the attack on Pearl Harbor; others can recall the precise moment when President Kennedy was shot. In my town, the tornado is our indelible moment, etched deep in our collective memory.

"It sounded like a train," everyone said of the tornado. That was our undoing. The Big Four rail line ran south of town. Accustomed to train noise, a goodly number of our citizens never sought shelter. Donald E.

Howard, fourteen, son of Mr. and Mrs. Homer Howard, was playing outside when the tornado hit and killed him. Two weeks later, volunteers began construction of a new home and storm cellar for the Howards. There are, however, some kinds of devastation that can never be repaired, and the loss of a child is one of them.

Bill Bair and his family owe their lives to a Maytag wringer washing machine. "We lived on High Street, in Doc Franz's old house. I was five years old, and we were eating supper when our front door blew open. My dad got up to close it and saw the tornado. He hustled us down the stairs into the cellar. We just made it. The tornado dropped the whole house right on top of us. A beam fell across our Maytag wringer washer, and we huddled under that. That Maytag washer held the house off us. Took my dad an hour to dig us out."

The tornado came out of the southwest after devastating Coatesville, killing fourteen, and demolishing the downtown. It careened across nine miles of woods and pastures, gathering steam, before striking Danville, surging across our northwest corner. All these years later, if one knows where to look, reminders abound, telltale clues of that dreadful day.

The Catholic rectory sits on the west side of town. It was, at one time, an elegant home, perhaps the finest residence in the area, and still retains a certain charm.

But if you were out for a walk one evening and paused to study it, you would notice something unusual about the house, a curious incompleteness. If you phoned the Bettys at *The Republican* newspaper—Betty Weesner and Betty Bartley—to ask why the rectory seems so peculiar, they would tell you the tornado sheared off the top floor, and it was never replaced.

While on that same walk, you would observe an interesting phenomenon. Sprinkled among stately Victorian homes are squat brick and limestone houses, built by gun-shy survivors of the '48 tornado. Their frame homes, reduced to kindling, were replaced by stout, thick-walled homes with deep basements.

Betty Weesner lives in one. When the Good Friday tornado barreled through, she was lying in her living room in a traction bed, swathed in a body cast, unable to escape. The upper story of the home collapsed, and the traction bed tilted, spilling her onto the floor and forming a protective niche where she lay until rescued.

Tom and Betsy Swords live a block and a half north of the courthouse on Washington Street, in a stately brick house built in the late 1840s by Christian C. Nave, the first lawyer in Danville. My friend Bill Eddy lived farther down that road. In my childhood, I rode my bicycle past the Swordses' on a regular basis without ever noticing the seam of brick where the east wall of the home had blown out. A photograph taken the day after the tornado shows the side of the home opened like a child's dollhouse, pictures still hanging squarely on the wall.

An automobile left for repair at the D&R gas station west of town was pushed down the road into town. Years later, an eyewitness reported that his lingering recollection of that day was seeing a car, driverless, rolling smartly down Main Street, never once crossing the center line.

Mrs. Wiley Dorset lived at 490 N. Jefferson Street and took shelter in her bathroom. The house was picked up and set down fifty yards away. When rescuers arrived, she was screaming in pain, but had no obvious wounds or fractures. The rise in air pressure had caused her corset to expand. While the corset was expanded, the rock-wool insulation from the house had blown underneath it. When the air pressure returned to normal, her corset contracted, trapping the insulation next to her skin and causing no small amount of discomfort. Stories soon circulated about Mrs. Dorset's corset.

In the days immediately following the tornado, Mrs. Blessing opened the Royal Theater, showing free movies for the children while their parents cleaned the town. This was back in the days before homeowner's insurance was widespread. Our one hotel was full, so neighbors took each other in until money could be raised and homes rebuilt.

My parents moved here in '57 and built a house without a basement, which struck the townspeople as sheer madness. My parents eventually came to their senses and bought a house with a basement, and so were well prepared for what came to be known as the Super Outbreak. On April 3, 1974, twenty tornadoes swept across Indiana just as we were sitting down for supper. If you were to consult a map of the Super Outbreak, you would see tornadoes on all sides of us, though not one of them touched down in our town. We lost trees and trash cans, but no lives or homes. The consensus of the coffee-shop crowd was that God, having punished us in '48, elected to spare us further tribulation.

All these years later, we are still vigilant. Each Friday at eleven o'clock, our fire department tests the storm siren. One can distinguish the Good Friday veterans from more recent arrivals by watching to see who twitches. The fire department used to sound the alarm at noon, smack in the middle of lunch, but it resulted in scalding burns as coffee cups all over town were overturned by jittery diners.

I've often heard the '48 tornado referred to as an "act of God." What a curious notion, that when God acts it is always calamitous. Why wasn't the generous outpouring to rebuild the Howard home called an act of God? Or Mrs. Blessing tending the town's children at the Royal? Or one family welcoming another into their home? What are those things, if not acts of God?

I suspect that in the days following the tornado, children overheard their parents discussing this "act of God" and were horrified that some crazed, ferocious deity could reach down and smite everyone and everything they loved. I wonder how long it took them to shed that image of the Divine, if they ever did. Perhaps even now they believe God will come again, visiting the earth with wind and fire, taking some and leaving others.

When I was a child, we had regular tornado drills at our school, long before the state required it. We would march single file into the hallway and sit with our backs to the wall, our heads between our legs, our hands covering our heads. We never knew whether it was a drill or the real thing and, until Mr. Michaels came on the intercom asking us to return to our rooms, we would scarcely breathe.

"What if this is a real tornado?" I once whispered to Bill Eddy, who was curled in a ball beside me. "How will we know?"

"It'll sound like a train," he whispered back. "They always sound like trains."

The State of Housing

I know a man who, after the death of his parents, in-
herited the home in which he'd grown up. It was not
an elegant home, but was sturdily built and had several
charms, chief among them a large porch and two hard
maple trees that hovered over the house, embracing it.
He and his wife moved in, applied a fresh coat of paint
inside and out, and spent many blissful years there
before he lost his job and fell on hard times. More ac-
curately, I suppose, hard times fell on him.

One day, in the newspaper, I saw the house listed
in a tax sale. The man and his wife had fallen behind
on their property taxes, and the sheriff had served a
notice of foreclosure. The next time I drove by, they
were holding a yard sale, selling off their belongings to
satisfy their tax bill and save their home.

I stopped to visit, poked among his goods, and thought of giving him the money to meet his debt, but I knew he wouldn't accept it. In addition to being poor, he was also proud. I bought a camping lantern and chair instead. His wife conducted the transaction. He stood behind her, toeing the ground, covered in sackcloth and ashes, too embarrassed to look at me.

A few months later, the house was sold at auction, and the man and his wife were cast out, their long years of pleasant residence, of cherishing old memories and making new ones, brought to an end.

The sheriff is not a cruel man. When the opportunity arose for me to speak with him, he reminded me he was an elected official, acting on my behalf. I'm all for the social compact and paying taxes, but I want no part of taking a man's home, of prying from his grasp the wall where his children's heights were recorded, of seizing the patch of flowers whose bulbs were transplanted from his grandmother's garden.

For years, my wife and I drifted from one rented space to another before we were able to afford our own home. My wife is skittish about borrowing money and preferred to save instead of borrow. The day we handed over the money and were given a key to the front door was a stellar moment for us, the start of a satisfying era.

Our home is by no means perfect, but it is ours, the stage for our dramas both tragic and comic.

Like any house, it has its faults, but none of them so significant we want to move. When the wind blows hard from the southwest and it rains, our kitchen roof leaks. I've hired three different men to patch it, with no success. I finally decided to fix it myself. I drove up to the city and bought a soup pot. I set it on the countertop whenever it rains.

While I'm enumerating its faults, I should also mention our house needs one more room. I'm not clear what that room should be; I just know I've often wished we had one more. I commandeered an upstairs bedroom for an office, so our son Spencer has to sleep downstairs in what would have been the laundry room, which we moved to the basement. Now my wife has to descend two flights of stairs whenever she does laundry. Consequently, she is trim and vigorous. I would do the laundry myself, but don't want to deprive her of beneficial exercise.

I was nosing around in the attic one day and found the blueprints of our home rolled up in a tube. According to them, a Mr. Russell Oatman from Massachusetts designed our home. I hope for his sake he never crosses paths with my wife. Our home also lacks a kitchen pantry. When we dream of having an extra room, that's the one she mentions.

There are several matters I'd like to raise with Mr. Oatman. We eat supper at six-thirty every evening, just as the sun is shining through our kitchen window. If Mr. Oatman had moved that window six inches to the north, it wouldn't shine in my eyes while I eat. Instead, I have to squint the whole time I'm eating. By the end of supper, I have a headache and am in a foul mood the rest of the evening. I'd like to ask Mr. Oatman what he was thinking when he put that window there.

As long as I was talking with Mr. Oatman, I'd ask him where he intended we place our Christmas tree. No matter where we put it, it's in the way. The entire month of December we have to squeeze past our tree to enter our living room. Each house should contain a spare corner for such things as a Christmas tree or the rocking chair you inherited from your grandmother. Ours doesn't, and I blame Mr. Oatman.

There are two hallways in the upstairs of our home—a front hallway and a rear hallway. The front hallway connects the two front bedrooms. When we first moved in, I installed a row of pegs in that hallway to hang our bathrobes on. I can't count the number of times I've stubbed my toe on the hall doorway while retrieving my robe in the middle of the night. If Mr. Oatman had moved that doorway even an inch, I would have been spared much pain these past seven years.

Across the road from our house lives a woman with six dogs. Our bedroom faces her farm, and her dogs have wakened me at all hours of the night. Why Mr. Oatman didn't put the master bedroom on the other side of the house facing our quiet neighbor is something I'd like to know.

Mr. Oatman was not having his best day when he designed our garage either. It is always a foot smaller than we need it to be. When I open the car door, it bangs against the wheelbarrow. I'm continually bumping into our riding lawn mower. In the drawings, Mr. Oatman referred to our garage as a two-and-a-half-car garage. I don't know where in the world he planned to put that extra half car. It takes all our effort to wedge two in there.

If Mr. Oatman and I ever meet, we'll have a lot to discuss.

Just so you don't have the impression Mr. Oatman was a complete flop, I want to mention what he did well. He excelled at fireplaces. We have three of them—one each in our living room, dining room, and kitchen. They draw perfectly, were beautifully designed and constructed, and have enhanced our lives immeasurably. In the middle of winter, when our town is seized in an icy grip, we build a fire on the kitchen hearth and thank the heavens for Mr. Oatman.

Mr. Oatman also understood proportion. Our house doesn't have a two-story entrance or ten-foot ceilings. There is ample storage, but not so much to encourage pack-ratting. The rooms are modest in number and size, the design simple, the construction sound. The windows are tight and well placed, with the exception of that one kitchen window. I don't want to let Mr. Oatman entirely off the hook, but most days I think highly of him.

No house is perfect. The average homeowner is constantly casting about for some improvement to make. But even the imperfections grow on us, and we don't part with them easily. My mother-in-law has lived in the same house since 1941. She hopes to die there, in her sleep, and I hope her wish is granted. Well-meaning people urge me to nudge her into a retirement home, but I'm generally opposed to separating folks from their homes for any reason, be it old age, tax delinquency, or to make way for a new highway. Homes aren't just brick and mortar; they are the repositories of our lives. We made love, war, and peace in their rooms. Every corner, every nook, every cranny prompts a memory. When the memory is peeled from us, so is the person.

Even our younger son, Sam, feels this attachment and can't imagine living anywhere else. "Can I live in the red house when I grow up?" he asks on a regular basis. We tell him he'll want to have his own red house then. He looks at us as if we're addlepated, as if he can't imagine any scenario that would compel him to leave this place.

I hope when my son needs a home, Mr. Oatman is still working. We'll sell our son this house and have Mr. Oatman build a new one just like it. Except this time we'll add a pantry, adjust the kitchen window and hall doorway, move the master bedroom around to the quiet side, and construct a larger garage. We'll add that extra room we've always wanted and put a fifth corner in the living room for our Christmas tree. Then we'll have the perfect house, and I can complain about something else.

Better Late Than Never!

Whe you're a minister, there are always ser-
mons you wish you could unpreach. In my first
church, I served under a kind soul named Keith Kirk.
I hadn't been there long when he fell sick the Sunday
before Thanksgiving and the task of preaching fell to
me. In my defense, I had only a few hours to prepare a
message, though even if I had had a week to get ready, I
would probably have given the same sermon.

All these years later, I remember the sermon with
stark clarity. After a joke or two to pacify the crowd,
who had come to hear Keith speak and were now faced
with a pale imitation, I launched into a series of ex-
hortations, ordering the congregation to be grateful,
lest God be angered by their ingratitude and zap them.
After the service, I stood at the door and shook hands

with everyone. They all commented on the weather, which I now understand meant the sermon was a flop. To the delight of everyone, Keith recovered quickly and I managed to avoid the pulpit for another year.

I bring this up because this sermon lives on, revived by a number of preachers, often around Thanksgiving. The sermons vary in eloquence, but the message is still the same—be grateful or else. When Abraham Lincoln formally established Thanksgiving, he probably didn't have in mind the arming of clerics, but that's precisely what's happened.

There is probably not one recorded instance of someone being grateful because they were ordered to, whether by a pastor or parent. This, however, does not prevent me from commanding my children to be grateful. Every night Joan and I insist our sons brush their teeth. In all the years we've done this, they've never thanked us for promoting dental hygiene. Someday they will be grateful they had parents who cared about such things, but today is not that day and no amount of haranguing them to be grateful will change that.

Here are some things I'm just now starting to appreciate:

I'm grateful my father warned against arrogance. I meet adults who think they're big shots, and they are insufferable.

I'm grateful my mother taught me to question religious claims. A lot of damage is done when we invest religious leaders with great power. A little skepticism in matters religious never hurts. Ditto for politics.

I'm grateful my parents taught me to measure people by how they treated those who served them. Beware of people who treat waiters and waitresses poorly. They'll treat you that way too.

I'm grateful my parents urged me to get a paper route when I was eleven. The job taught me responsibility and not to despise the poor, who were usually more generous with their tips than my wealthy customers.

I'm grateful my parents had me. I once told them I didn't ask to be born, but now I'm glad they didn't wait for my permission. Life has its difficult moments, but it also holds deep joys, such as springtime and children and the day after Christmas.

I'm grateful Joan's parents taught her not to choose a husband based on his looks.

I've been fired from two jobs in my life. I never bothered to thank the people who fired me, even though getting fired enabled me to move on to better things.

Emily Post and Ann Landers encourage us to express our thanks as close to the kind deed as possible. That is a generally sound idea, but it's conditioned us to believe that delayed gratitude lacks sincerity. I've found just the opposite to be true. A man once showed up on my doorstep to thank me for a small kindness I had shown him years before. My gesture, which seemed trifling at the time, turned out to have had a significant and beneficial effect on his life. So he came to my house to express his gratitude. His appreciation was heartfelt, and I was touched by it.

I don't contradict Emily Post and Ann Landers lightly, but as with any rule of conduct it's the spirit of the law that matters. Occasionally, time provides perspective; what seemed like cruelty years ago turned out to be a kindness.

When I was twenty-one, I began dating a lovely young woman. She was attractive, bright, and articulate. For a few beguiling months, her charm was such that I would have happily married her, had I sensed interest on her part. But the attraction was one-sided, and she dropped me. For some time, a cloud followed me wherever I went, drenching me with the bitter rain of broken dreams.

Then I met my wife, who is also attractive, bright, and articulate. Plus kind and charitable, and nice to children, animals, wayfaring strangers, and one dense husband.

I recall my former love with a mix of fondness and curiosity. I have no idea what happened to her. Our severance was quick and clean, and I haven't seen her since. When she broke up with me, my mother told me I should be grateful, that a bad breakup beat a bad marriage. But the pain was too fresh, and I was in no mood for thankfulness. Now, twenty-four years later, I am deeply grateful. If our paths should ever cross, I intend to thank her for tossing me aside. Though I didn't realize it at the time, I landed on a soft pillow.

This is the irony of gratitude—we're often less inclined to express it when, in retrospect, it is the most deserved.

Exercise and Other
Dirty Words

Several years ago, my wife began subscribing to a magazine that routinely contained offensive, distasteful language. Copies of the magazine were soon strewn about the house—next to her chair, on the kitchen table, atop the nightstand next to our bed.

My polite requests that they be discarded fell on deaf ears.

"What's wrong with my magazines?" she asked.

I told her I found the language in them repulsive.

"What language?" she asked.

"All those dirty words."

"What dirty words? I don't know what you're talking about."

It was just as I had feared. Constant exposure to foul language had desensitized her. I picked up a magazine and thumbed through it. It didn't take long to spy an offending word. "Right there," I said, pointing.

"*Exercise* is not a dirty word," she said.

"Then how about that one," I asked, jabbing at the word *calisthenics*. There were other words in her magazine too disgusting to mention.

Despite my protests, she continued to leave the magazines in plain sight, even circling articles and leaving them where I couldn't help but notice.

It's been said that you don't know a person until you marry her. That is certainly true in my case. My wife was a sweet, reasonable person when I married her, but in the past ten years or so, she's become a fanatic. She exercises constantly, walking four miles each day. Once, I accompanied her, on a pleasant, summer evening after the heat had broken. Within a few blocks, it was clear we had different expectations. I was under the impression we were taking a stroll, while she believed we were on the Bataan Death March.

"Walk faster," she barked.

"What's the hurry?" I asked. "Can't we just enjoy ourselves?"

Several of our neighbors were out working in their yards. I slowed down to visit with them.

"Just wave and keep on walking," she hissed. "Do not stop."

I began to fear for my safety. She appeared to want to strike me in the kneecap, crippling me, leaving me along the road to die. I saw her glancing about for a stout stick with which to clout me.

That night, while lying in bed, after she'd fallen asleep, I suggested, softly, that we not take any more walks together. It was all for naught. When I awoke the next morning, there was a box of granola on the kitchen table.

"Where are my Cocoa Krispies?" I asked.

"In the trash. From now on, it's healthy food and exercise for you. Eat up. You're going to need your strength."

We walked three miles that day. It was absolutely dreadful. I broke at the two-mile marker, pleading with her to turn back, get the car, and drive me home.

"Absolutely not."

We were out front of Ron Randolph's home. "How about I see if Ron can drive me home?"

"Stop your whining."

I walked again the next day, and the day after that.

That was five years ago, and I've walked three miles a day ever since, for a total of three thousand two hundred and eighty-five miles, roughly the distance from my front door to the country of Panama.

The weather is beautiful down here, and until my wife comes to her senses, I have no intention of going home.

My Conflicted Life

When we bought our home, the realtor told us it had four bedrooms. We only found three, and suspected the kitchen fireplace was the fourth. Our second winter in the house, we installed a woodstove in the fireplace, mostly to fill the space.

A man came out from the city, wrestled the woodstove into place, hooked it up to the chimney, then gave us a few simple but important instructions—*Do not touch the stove while it is hot! Do not pour gasoline into the stove! If the stove blows up, vacate the premises immediately!* He regaled us with stories of entire towns obliterated by exploding stoves, of families left to wander destitute among the ruins. "Quite frankly," the woodstove man said, "I'm surprised they're not against the law."

We eyed the stove warily for the next several months, in much the same way citizens of ancient Pompeii kept tabs on Mount Vesuvius. But in mid-January, when a snowstorm barged in, we lost power and our heat with it.

My wife, reckless woman that she is, suggested we fire up the woodstove. My faculties weakened by the cold, I agreed. Within an hour our house was toasty warm. By the third hour we had changed into our bathing suits and were sipping margaritas and listening to Don Ho sing "Tiny Bubbles" on his *Hawaiian Favorites* album. Our neighbors, mad with envy, peered through our windows, their noses blackened by frostbite, their eyebrows crusted with frost.

That was seven years ago, and we've heated with wood ever since. I have mixed feelings about our woodstove. A fan of trees, I worry we are cutting down too many of them, but now I'm addicted to burning oak logs in our woodstove. I spend entire evenings in front of it, mulling over the clash of my passions.

I was discussing my moral dilemma with my friend Jim, who, like me, is a pastor and writer, and an ethicist to boot. He visits my house every Thursday through the winter to write books with me. We work upstairs, but he uses any excuse to slip downstairs and stand with his back to the fireplace.

"I love woodstoves," he said one particularly bitter day. "This is the warmest I've been in days."

"It is nice," I agreed. "But I hate the idea of cutting down trees. I'm thinking of giving up my woodstove."

He looked slightly panicked.

"Do you personally cut down the trees?" he asked.

I explained that I purchased my firewood from a veneer mill, that it consisted of the leftover tops from veneer logs.

"Well, there you go," Jim said. "They've already cut down the trees. You're just making sure they don't go to waste."

I had never thought of it that way.

It's been a real blessing having an ethicist for a friend. A clever ethicist can justify just about anything. Jim has changed my mind about a number of subjects, causing me to do things I used to think were wrong, including voting for Democrats.

Several years ago, when Senator John Kerry ran for president, he was accused of flip-flopping. That was supposed to make us suspicious of him, make us think he couldn't be trusted to stand firm. It had just the opposite effect on me. I admired him all the more. In him, I saw a kindred spirit—a lover of trees and woodstoves, willing to wrestle with the contradiction.

Our world is cursed with an abundance of leaders who never change their minds though a mountain of evidence proves them wrong. I'm growing fond of the conflicted man, and the doubting woman, for that matter. (I don't give two hoots about gender, but am partial to competence.) Although fence-sitters can be exasperating, people whose minds are set in stone can be dangerous. All tyrants have this in common—they are certain they are right, can't be persuaded otherwise, and will take up the sword to prove their point. Say what you will about us flip-floppers, we seldom start wars.

This is my conflicted life—sitting beside my woodstove on a winter's evening, writing a letter to the editor bemoaning the slaughter of trees. If I were a purist, this contradiction would bother me. Since I'm a flip-flopper, I go merrily on, not letting the burr of inconsistency prod too deeply.

Too Many Friends

Every year or so, I read a story in the newspaper about someone dying friendless and penniless. The penniless part I understand, what with the health care industry doing all it can to separate us from our money. But the friendless part mystifies me.

I'm not bragging, but I've always had a knack for making friends. It began when I was a teenager and I started asking girls to go out on dates. They would smile, then say, "Let's just be friends." I've been making friends ever since.

I have so many friends, I can't begin to stay in touch with all of them. As I write this, a stack of twenty-three letters sits on my desk, awaiting my response. I was taught that personal letters should be handwritten, so I will spend six hours answering those letters. Each of those friends will write back, plus a few others, and I'll be in the same boat as before—too many friends and not enough time. The poet Sam Foss once wrote, "Let me live in my house by the side of the road and be a friend to man." That's a fine sentiment and makes for good poetry. I just hope Sam Foss has a lot of stationery and nothing else that needs doing.

My surplus of friends has nothing to do with personal charm or likeability, but with my age. I've been alive long enough to have made a lot of friends, but I'm not so old they're starting to die off. In the past five years, I've probably made fifty new friends, but have lost only three. I'm a victim of statistical probability. When I age, this problem will remedy itself, but until then I'm burdened with an excess of relationships that are depleting my energy and spare time.

I've been thinking of doing something scandalous so all but my closest friends will desert me. It would have to be something appropriately disgraceful, perhaps even illegal, which would get me arrested. People heading for prison shed friends like a dog sheds hair.

There are other ways to get rid of friends. Letting it be known we need help moving causes even our most stalwart friends to flee. With all the friends I have, one would think a few of them would volunteer to help split and stack my firewood every spring, but they desert me in droves.

Discussing religion is also a good way to drop friends. I once wrote a controversial book in which I stated my belief in universal salvation. Several of my friends thought I'd gone off the theological deep end and stopped talking to me. But other people read the book and began attending my church. Within a few months, I'd replaced all the friends I'd lost and added an extra dozen. Perhaps if I wrote a book against motherhood, it would make everyone mad at me and I wouldn't be so busy.

A couple times a month, I go somewhere to give a speech. The secret to giving a good speech is making it easy for people to like you. The only problem is that by the end of the speech, you've made even more friends. I'm thinking of giving up the speech racket and selling insurance. Besides going to jail, there's no quicker way to lose friends than pestering them to buy something.

In addition to my church friends, I have family friends, childhood friends, neighborhood friends, out-of-state friends, motorcycling friends, publishing friends, e-mail friends, coffee-shop friends, and dear, dear friends I've never met. From time to time, someone will approach me and announce that we have a mutual friend. They then mention a name I've never heard. "She told me you are dear, dear friends." I smile, nod my head, and say, "Oh, yes, how is Margaret? Please give her my best." It used to be people had to know one another to be dear, dear friends, but the standards appear to have slipped.

My son Sam keeps his list of friends trimmed to a few carefully chosen boys with whom he passes his days. If a friend should move, creating an opening on his list, Sam never hastens to fill the vacancy, nor does he trust in circumstance to plug the hole. Instead, he scrutinizes the roll of potential friends as a jeweler might study a gem. But while the jeweler looks for color, cut, and clarity, Sam focuses on temperament, range of interests, and faithfulness, then makes his choice, and sticks to it. He approaches friendship more diligently than most people approach marriage.

If we are known by the company we keep, my son has been more zealous of his reputation than most. I admire his discretion—that he hasn't confused breadth of friendship with depth of friendship, that he loves a few people deeply rather than all the world poorly.

Each year, *Forbes* magazine lists the hundred richest people. I don't know why we measure a person's wealth in terms of dollars, when we all know the richest people are those with loyal friends.

Professional Thinkers

I've always enjoyed meeting new people, except for the awkward first moments, when we sniff each other over, asking questions of one another, trying to place the other in a convenient pigeonhole. I was at a dinner party not long ago, and a man asked me what I did. I knew he wasn't inquiring about my hobbies or daily functions, but about my vocations, which are numerous, but always lead to a dead end. If I say I'm a pastor, people find someone else to talk with. If I tell them I'm a writer, they haven't read my books. If I tell them I'm a speaker, they want me to speak to their garden club or bowling league.

So I thought for a moment, then said, "I'm a professional thinker." The answer intrigued him, and we went on to have a fascinating conversation, then made plans for lunch the following week.

Though professional thinkers ponder a variety of subjects, I confine most of my thinking to God. Occasionally, I will turn my thoughts to world affairs or politics or the peculiarities of people. I've never invented anything new to think about. Often, after I've given a speech, someone in the audience will approach me and say, "I've thought that way for years." Clearly, my thinking isn't original if other people have been thinking that way too. The only difference is that I get paid.

You would think that since I'm a professional thinker, my thoughts would be superior to everyone else's. Professional athletes, for example, get paid for doing something better than the rest of us. But professional thinkers don't necessarily think better than amateur thinkers. Our knack is in convincing others we do.

I do most of my thinking in the morning and late afternoon. If I try to think after lunch, I fall asleep. I've been known to think in the middle of the night. Then I have to get out of bed and walk down the hallway to my office to write down what I thought, so I don't forget it. Though I'm good at thinking, I'm not an accomplished rememberer.

Unlike my dinner-party friend, many people are wary of professional thinkers, dismissing us as eggheads or ivory-tower liberals. It isn't unusual to see well-educated politicians, believing voters will resent their intellect, behave like simpletons to get elected. I'm a populist to the core, but I don't want Jethro Bodine running our country.

To the casual observer, thinking looks suspiciously like sitting around doing nothing. I do some of my best thinking in my recliner. But someone walking past my home might glance through my living-room window, see me sitting there with my eyes closed, and think to themselves, *There's that Gulley, sitting on his rear end again. Boy, I wish I had a job like that.* They don't realize I'm breaking a sweat thinking.

Professional thinkers even come under attack by their own family members. When we were leaving the dinner party, I backed into another car after my wife had warned me it was there. "And you call yourself a professional thinker," she said.

I've been fired twice during my long career as a professional thinker for thinking thoughts my bosses didn't want me to think. The first time was from a church that didn't like what I thought about hell. The second time was from a publisher that didn't like what I thought about heaven. When it comes to religion, professional thinkers can't win for losing. Each time I found a new job within a few hours. That's the advantage of being a professional thinker—there is never a shortage of thoughts that need thinking.

Despite our need for professional thinkers, our country has lately been relying too heavily on amateur thinkers. They populate radio, television, and the Internet, spewing their invective in the name of wisdom and common sense. Though wearing the guise of the thinker, they care less about knowledge and more about propaganda, trading in the party line, the half-truth, the telling wink. They speak with forked tongues and crossed fingers, ask God to bless their efforts, wrap the flag about their shoulders, and then strangle the freedoms they claim to love.

There ought to be a law that all thinkers, professional and otherwise, must foreswear all allegiances, resign from all factions and parties, and abandon all preconceptions before undertaking their work. Except for me, of course, who alone of all the professional thinkers is able to remain above the coarse partisanship of human exchange.

Zipper

After pastoring a Quaker meeting in the city for eight years, I took down my ministerial shingle, returned to my hometown with my family, bought a house, and laid out of church for a year to write and pummel the house into shape. It takes a while to personalize a home; a hundred different alterations are needed to suit the routine and spirit of the new dweller.

In an effort to help us, a friend gave us a book about feng shui—the Chinese art of positioning furniture and objects to balance their positive and negative energies and ensure harmonious living. I sat on the living-room floor, cross-legged in the yoga position, humming and chanting, my open hands resting on my knees. I announced to my wife that the picture of her Aunt Edna was emitting negative energy.

But there was a lack to the house, an emptiness around the edges I couldn't name. Then one winter afternoon I was seated in front of our woodstove, rocking back and forth, and the thought struck me how pleasant it would be to have a dog stretched out on the rug before me, the both of us gazing at the fire and thinking of dinner.

"We need a dog," I said.

"No, we don't," my wife said firmly, which meant I would have to resort to subterfuge.

The next Sunday morning I was scheduled to speak at a rural Quaker meeting fifty miles from home. My wife walked me to my truck, kissed me good-bye, and warned me not to bring home a dog.

"What if I come across a soft little puppy abandoned in a ditch, shivering in the cold and starving to death?" I asked her. "What if a pack of coyotes are circling it, ready to attack? What if it's lying in the middle of the road, too exhausted to move, and a semi is bearing down on it? Would you prefer I leave it there?"

No response, just a frown.

On the way to the meetinghouse, I passed a puppies-for-sale sign. I made a mental note of its location, then proceeded to the church, where I delivered a sermon to a congregation so lethargic they needed dusting. At the conclusion of worship, an elderly farmer approached me. He reached into the chest pocket of his over-alls, pulled out the church's bankbook, and extracted seventy-five dollars. "That's the most we've ever paid a preacher," he announced. "Personally, I don't think it was worth it."

One develops a thick hide after years of being a pastor, particularly if one meddles as much as I do, so his assessment of my preaching didn't trouble me. I smiled, thanked him for the honorarium, climbed into my truck, and made a beeline for the puppies for sale.

I had long been opposed to paying for a dog. A number of dogs populated my childhood, not one of them purchased, each of whom earned its keep by being good company, disposing of the table scraps, and guarding the homestead. This was back in the days when dogs wandered at will, like gypsies moving from place to place, in constant search of a better deal.

In my childhood, dogs were scrutinized carefully by the potential owner. Did he have fleas? Was she pregnant? Was her disposition pleasant? Was he good with children? It was the dog who had to pass muster. It's different today. When I first thought of getting a dog, I visited the animal shelter and was given a test to determine my fitness for pet ownership. Would I be home during the day? Had I ever been charged with neglect? Did I have the financial means to provide for a dog?

Would my children be kind to the pet? Did I have any other pets that might make the dog anxious?

The people from the animal shelter wanted to visit our home before approving the adoption. Presidential candidates receive less scrutiny than people wanting a dog from the pound. Then, and I still can't figure this out, if the pound determines the dog might not be safe in your care and no one else adopts it, they gas it.

So I turned to free enterprise in search of a dog.

There were five puppies for sale—rat terriers—four males who yipped and yapped and jumped all over me, as boys are prone to do, and one calm, dignified female, hanging back, surveying her brothers as if embarrassed by their behavior.

I feel the same way about dogs as I do about my parishioners—I prefer freethinkers to fawners.

"I'll take that one," I told the farmer's wife, pointing to the female. "How much is she?"

"One hundred dollars," she said.

I told her I only had seventy-five, then asked if I could send her a check for the balance.

She studied the dog. "Don't bother. She's a little runty anyway. Seventy-five is fine."

If the dog was offended, she showed no sign of it. She seemed to sense a transaction had transpired, walked to my truck, and waited for me to lift her in, where she took her place beside me as gracefully and naturally as a queen ascending her throne.

We discussed names on the way home. I am under the firm conviction that dogs should have a say in their name, so we batted several back and forth before settling on Zipper.

"Yes," she said, "I like that. It denotes a certain zest for life, but is also distinctive."

It was the custom of my boys at that time to run from the house and greet me when I pulled in the driveway. So when Spencer, then six years old, tugged open the truck door, Zipper tumbled out into his arms. There was, when boy met dog, a look on their faces of pure, transcendent joy—the dog, at having secured a boy; the boy, at having secured a dog.

A veterinarian friend of ours urged us to attend a training class with Zipper, which we did to good effect. We are now perfectly trained. Zipper, however, does as she pleases, selects where and with whom she will sleep, brings every conversation around to herself, and insists on sitting in the front seat and picking the music when we ride in the car.

She is especially obstinate about using the rest room. She will hold her bowels for hours, even days, waiting for a weather front to advance; then when the storm is at its peak, she will demand we take her outside. If the weather is particularly foul, she will linger, sniffing every blade of grass until we are chilled to the bone.

As for her morality, it is noticeably deficient. She steals constantly, stashing our valuables under chairs and beds or burying them in the yard. She is a vandal, tipping over wastebaskets, chewing holes in blankets, and gnawing on furniture. She even looks like a criminal. Her eyes are close and hooded, her nose pointed, her expression cunning.

Her work ethic is also dreadful. She knows nothing about reciprocity and feels no obligation to pull her own weight. Each day, for nearly seven years, she has lain at my feet while I work, never once lifting a pampered paw to help. When we take her for a walk, she fakes a limp and insists on being carried.

Zipper is a traitor of the first order. Were a burglar to rob our house, she would greet him warmly and help haul the loot to his car.

She shuns all religious endeavors, has never stepped foot in a church, and is stingy in her support of the widow and orphan.

Other than these deficiencies, she has been a fine addition to our family and has several noble qualities. She has an unerring instinct for human hurt and, with one moistened paw to the wind, can sense which person most needs her gifts of consolation. She will do anything for a laugh, sports a perpetual grin, and loves a good joke.

She has an amazing tolerance for dull visitors. Long after our interest in a guest has waned, she is circling them, breaching their defenses to climb on their lap and share a story or two.

She is the picture of discretion. She once saw me naked exiting the bathtub, never told a soul, and has never raised the matter.

Zipper and I have a secret we've never told anyone. When my wife and sons leave the house each morning, Zipper and I curl up on the chair in front of the wood-stove and snooze. We don't sleep well at night. She's pacing the floors, and I'm sniffing for smoke and listening for burglars. And so on winter mornings, the sky still dark, the fire fending off the creeping cold, we nap, my dog and I, the edges of our lives now nicely filled.

The Writing Life

Have you ever noticed how many writers write books about writing? My grandfather worked in a glass factory for thirty-nine years. The last thing he wanted to talk about was working in a glass factory. I once spent a summer picking up roadkill. I have no desire to write a book about roadkill retrieval and disposal. There are some career choices that beg not to be written about. That writers want to write about writing speaks well of the vocation and the esteem in which it is held by those who practice it.

It was never my intention to be a writer. I stumbled into this paradise. The Quaker meeting I was pastoring began a newsletter and assigned the front page to me. Several years later, a friend introduced me to a publisher who asked to see the essays I'd written. I'd saved them in a shoebox. I mailed them to the publisher in Oregon, and six months later my first book came out.

And so I was a writer, to the utter amazement of every English teacher I'd ever had.

People often ask me how to get a book published. If there's a formula for such things, I've not found it. I've relied on dumb luck and divine intervention, both of which have served me well. But I suspect the best way to get a book published is to write a good book. The best way to write a good book is to read Strunk and White's *The Elements of Style* and do what it says. I'm a fundamentalist about few things, but *The Elements of Style* is gospel to me.

If you're going to be a writer, it helps to write things others want to read, but a gifted writer can make any subject interesting. One of the finest books I've read, *The Undertaking* by Thomas Lynch, is about being a mortician. Preparing people for burial doesn't ordinarily grab my attention, but Tom Lynch made the subject, pardon the pun, come alive for me. E. B. White caused countless *New Yorker* readers to dream of raising chickens, and Bill Bryson, in his book *The Mother Tongue,* wrote a chapter about cussing that grabbed this pastor's attention.

The key to good writing, assuming ability is present, is sticking to what fascinates you. If you aren't taken with your subject, readers won't be either. Write your passion. Writers are bombarded with requests from readers, editors, and publishers to write a particular kind of book. Books written to satisfy someone else end up satisfying no one. A man wrote me regularly demanding I write a book about sin. I told him if he was interested in sin, he should write his own book. I didn't know whether he was for sin or against it; he never said, and I didn't ask, for fear of exciting him further.

People requiring regular guidance and praise should find another way to earn their living. Writers are like explorers of old—sent off to explore strange lands, inadequately supplied, and quickly forgotten. When a writer discovers a new land, someone else gets the credit, usually the actor who starred in the movie. Say the words *Forrest Gump* and Tom Hanks springs to mind. But mention its author, Winston Groom, and people think of cigarettes.

Though most writers toil in obscurity, it's a hard vocation to top. The commute is easy. It is twenty-one feet from my bed to my office. Most mornings I detour through the kitchen, adding a flight of stairs and forty or so paces to the trip, which is still tolerable. I can wear whatever I wish to work, with little regard for current fashions or personal hygiene. Indeed, the more eccentric I look, the more mussed I appear, the more inclined people are to think I'm a genius. No one ever told Einstein to comb his hair. Writing is a great job for sloppy people like me.

Because I know how pleasurable writing can be, I'm not at all surprised so many people want to do it. On an almost weekly basis someone hands me a manuscript they've written and asks me to read it, urging me to be brutally honest. The first few times that happened, I was flattered they wanted my opinion and devoted many hours evaluating their material. It didn't take long to learn people didn't want my honest opinion as much as they wanted me to tell them their manuscript was wonderful. Now when people give me something to read, I set it aside for a week, then write them a letter advising them to keep at it. I never specify whether they should keep at it because their work shows promise or needs practice. I let them interpret my counsel however they wish.

People who write for a living are annoyed when others do it poorly. A restaurant owner in our town writes his own menu, which overflows with grammatical errors and misspelled words. The food is good, but I read the menu and lose my appetite. I once offered, as kindly as I could, to edit his menu, but he declined, saying it was fine the way it was. But proper English isn't a matter of opinion, and sincerity counts for nothing. When a student says two plus three equals four, we mark him wrong, while letting poor grammar stand. Attitudes like this drive writers crazy.

Occasionally, I travel somewhere to speak about writing. If teenagers are present, they invariably ask how much money I make. The adults blush at such brazenness, though it doesn't prevent them from paying careful attention to my response. Most folks labor under the delusion that writers are a prosperous lot. I tell them, "Not nearly as much as you think."

Writing, I've learned, is a communal activity. It's not unusual, when I go into town to the store, for someone to ask, "When's our next book coming out?"

"This summer," I tell them, giving them a thumbs-up.

I'm pleased my fellow citizens feel a part of the enterprise. They are in my mind as I write. The peculiarities of my characters are their peculiarities—their mannerisms, their fears, their likes and dislikes, their more virtuous qualities. They sense the collaboration. A few of them have even suggested I share the royalties. Ray Whitaker, who works for the town street department, announces, whenever he sees me, "There's the man who made a million dollars writing about me and didn't give me a dime of it."

It's sad to consider how many people don't like what they do. I have met disgruntled taxi drivers, disillusioned teachers, and disheartened physicians. But all the writers I've ever met loved their vocation. Although I try to avoid generalizations, it seems accurate to say that the world would be a happier place if everyone was a writer.

My Wife, the Scofflaw

Several summers ago, my wife and I rented a motor home to visit Mount Rushmore with our sons. Our first day on the road was an advertisement on wheels. Joan looked attractive in her summer outfit; our boys were well-groomed, polite, and happy. I had the serene appearance of a seasoned traveler.

The first night, at a small campground in Creston, Iowa, Joan and I stayed up talking and eating ice cream from the RV freezer, like traveling royalty.

"This is the way to go," I said to Joan. "We ought to buy one."

"Why do we have to own one?" she asked. "Why can't we just rent one? It's a lot cheaper."

"Yeah, but if we owned it, it would be ours," I pointed out.

I often make undeniably true statements to confound my wife.

She sat quietly, eating her ice cream. "It seems good to be able to enjoy something without having to own it," she said after a while.

Whenever my wife sits quietly, thinking, I know the news is going to be bad.

The next evening we stopped in Chamberlain, South Dakota, and camped alongside the Missouri River, where we rented a motorboat.

"Let's buy a boat!" the boys said that night around the campfire.

"Yes, let's!" I agreed.

Joan sat there, thinking quietly. "If we owned a boat, we'd be too busy taking care of it to enjoy it. Renting one occasionally is much wiser."

There was no stopping my wife's descent into madness.

I have no one but myself to blame. When we were first married, I regularly extolled the virtues of simplicity, though I had no intention of making simplicity a lifelong pursuit. I was only for it because I was broke, a situation I intended to remedy. Now we're in taller cotton, but my wife still appreciates the minimalist approach to life.

I don't understand Joan's aversion to ownership. It strikes me as anti-American, and I question her patriotism daily. If we spend a week in a cabin, it is enough for her to simply enjoy the experience. I want to buy a cabin.

If I sit in a comfortable chair, I want to buy one just like it. We have sixty-four chairs because of my commitment to a robust economy. This is a rating of 16 CPFM (chairs per family member).

After those religious fundamentalists attacked us and we went to war, President Bush urged us to invest in America and go shopping. I was all for it, but Joan wouldn't hear of it. With the government listening to our phone calls, I know somebody somewhere has to be writing down the names of people who won't do their patriotic duty and buy things. I told Joan she better watch it, but she just laughed. The scofflaw.

It was her idea for us to visit Mount Rushmore. She told me she wanted us to enjoy a place I could never own.

But the first thing the park ranger leading our tour said was that Mount Rushmore belonged to the American people. "To you, and you, and you," she said, pointing directly at me. Then she said Abraham Lincoln's face had a crack in it and that one day his nose will fall off.

"Great," I thought, "I've only owned it a day, and it already needs fixing."

Maybe Joan has a point. Maybe it's enough to enjoy something without having to possess it.

To enjoy a forest without having to own the trees.

To appreciate a fine chair without having to buy it.

To savor an experience with God without insisting others must encounter God the same way.

Hmm. I think I'll go sit in one of my sixty-four chairs and think about this some more.

The Death of Freedom

I was dragged kicking and screaming into the computer age. I wrote with a hunk of charcoal on slate for as long as I could before making my peace with modernity and buying a computer. Things went well for several years, and then my computer crashed, bringing my life to a shuddering halt. My initial response was panic, with occasional thoughts of suicide. But by the third day I'd recovered and was beginning to enjoy my technological respite.

I get a lot of e-mails from people asking me to do things for them—send a book here, give a speech there. With my computer down, I was sheltered from these demands and able to get caught up. I straightened my office, answered mail, and thought seriously about cleaning the fence row behind my house.

A new computer now sits on my desk. It is sleek and black and a gazillion times faster than my old one. A technician came out from the city to install it and transfer the data from my old computer to my new one.

He asked what I did for a living. I told him I was a Quaker pastor, and he began talking about religion. I sensed he wasn't religious himself, but some people think that's the only thing ministers can talk about, so off he went, careening down the theological trail.

"I'm a religious man myself," he said. "I don't believe in evolution."

"Excuse me?" I said.

"I don't believe in evolution," he repeated.

Despite zealous efforts by Christian fundamentalists to convince us otherwise, evolution poses no threat to healthy religion. Scientific knowledge is a threat to irrational religion, which might be why fundamentalists don't care for it.

"Why don't you believe in evolution?" I asked.

"Cause the monkeys are still here. Now if we're descended from monkeys, why are the monkeys still here?"

He hovered over my computer, working at a blinding pace, fingering the keyboard like a concert pianist. I wondered how someone could be so smart about one thing and so willfully ignorant about another.

But what troubled me even more was his assumption that because I was a Christian, I didn't believe in science. Here stood a man whose very livelihood depended on scientific endeavor, dismissing it out of hand, and thinking that because I was a person of faith, I couldn't appreciate the gains of science.

Religion has not been a good neighbor to science. First, there was that little dustup in 1633, when Galileo had the audacity to suggest that the earth revolved around the sun. The church, galled by such impudence, forced him to recant and placed him under house arrest for the remainder of his life. To its credit, the church admitted it was mistaken and apologized to Galileo, three hundred and fifty-nine years later, in 1992.

Then Charles Darwin suggested plants and animals could adapt to a changing environment. A reasonable statement on the face of it, it's caused hundreds of thousands of Christians to pull their children out of public schools rather than expose them to this heresy. I'm not sure who'll invent the cure for cancer, discover a new energy source, or genetically engineer a plant that will end starvation, but I bet it won't be an anti-Darwinian Christian.

If we were to ask these religionists why they resist scientific advancement, they would claim to be guarding the truth. But the enemies of truth are, and always have been, ignorance and intolerance.

History has shown that there are two ways to destroy a nation. It can either be bombed back to the Stone Age or handed over to fundamentalists who then do what they do best—dismantle progress, condemn the curious, demonize women and homosexuals, and crush dissent—all the while claiming to be victims of religious bigotry when others seek to curb their excesses.

This was not the religion of my childhood, when church members served on the local school board out of a sense of civic obligation, not because they wanted to teach creationism and require children to pray. Compulsive prayer is the canary in the cage; when prayer is compelled, Inquisitions are close behind.

Time and again, we have seen it—that the death of science is the death of freedom.

What is science, but that noble effort to unlock the mysteries of God's creation? Where does evil lurk in that? Doesn't our growing knowledge deepen our appreciation of divine creativity? And if the opposite is true, if in some laboratory a scientist concludes the Bible is mistaken and there is no God, what is that to me? The freedom that permits me to believe in God grants the scientist the privilege not to. If I restrict his or her freedom, I inevitably limit my own. Tyranny is like the rabid dog that finally bites its master.

I was going to explain all this to the man working on my computer, but I needed my computer fixed and wanted to stay on his good side, so I let it pass. I hope he reads this though and concludes, as I have, that being descended from beasts is better than being ruled by them.

Simplicity

Several years ago, with the holidays rushing toward me, I vowed not to overschedule the month of December. "If anyone calls and asks me to do something, I'm going to tell them no," I said to Joan.

The next morning the phone rang. "How would you like to go to sunny Florida in early December?" my publisher asked. "We need you to give a speech at a booksellers convention."

"Sure," I said.

That afternoon, the telephone rang again. It was a pastor, asking if I could speak at his church one evening in December.

"I'd be happy to," I said.

A few hours later, some Quakers from Ohio e-mailed, wanting to meet with me to talk about Jesus. I'm not sure why they couldn't find someone in Ohio to talk with about Jesus, but I enjoy theological discourse, so I agreed to meet them.

Later that night, an old friend phoned to see how I was doing. I hadn't seen him for years and hadn't given him much thought. We all have old friends, former classmates or neighbors, we no longer stay in touch with and are content to keep it that way. We haven't stopped liking them, but there are only so many hours in the day. If we bump into them, the protocol is unspoken but understood. One or the other will say it's a shame we don't see one another more often, and the other will say, "Yes, we need to get together." The first person understands this is just a pleasantry, not an invitation.

But my old friend on the phone has always been a bit dense, and he said, "Hey, that'd be great. When do you want to get together?"

"How about in December?" I suggested.

"I can't wait," he said.

My brother-in-law called the next day. "If I bring Mom up, can she stay with you the first week of December and then you drive her back home?"

"Fine with me," I said.

A few hours later, a bookstore owner called to ask if I could do a book signing at her store.

"When?" I asked.

"December 7."

"Works for me," I said.

Steve Newman, from the Rotary Club, phoned the week before Thanksgiving. "Could you speak at our December Rotary meeting? We'll buy your lunch."

"Sounds good," I told him.

The next morning, a woman from my alma mater called to see if I could speak at the college's Christmas party.

"I'd be honored."

My publisher phoned later that day with the cheerful news that he had signed me up for thirty-five radio interviews during the month of December. "Isn't that great?!" he said.

"Simply wonderful."

"By the way," he said. "We might need you to go to Los Angeles for a few days."

"Okay."

Then an acquaintance called to ask if I could speak at his club's Christmas party the Sunday night before Christmas.

I explained that I reserved Sunday afternoons and evenings for my family.

"Bring them along," he said. "You'll have a ball."

Attending a Christmas party at a club I didn't like enough to join in the first place is not my idea of fun.

"No thank you. But I appreciate your thinking of me."

"You have to come," he said, starting to sound irritated. "I already told them you'd accepted."

"I can maybe stop by for a half hour," I said. I'd tell my family I was using the bathroom. They probably wouldn't even notice I was gone.

I'm grateful I belong to a religious tradition that encourages simplifying our lives so we can make time for the things that matter. I hate to think how busy I'd be if I weren't a simple Quaker. I'd probably fill my calendar with all manner of things. It's a good thing I'm so disciplined.

I'd write more about this, but my phone is ringing and I need to answer it.

The Natural Order
of Things

Things are more complicated now than when I was a kid. It's no longer clear on whose side we belong. When I was a kid it was the children versus the adults. Every grown-up in town conspired to rein me in. They felt free to correct, coerce, and otherwise control me. If I was doing something I shouldn't have been doing, Eddy Swanson's mother was just as likely to box my ears as my own mother. It wasn't that I was singularly bad; this was just the accepted custom. Adults and children were at odds—everyone knew it, accepted it as inevitable, and was faithful to their assigned role. We children tried to get away with whatever we could, and it was the adults' job to see that we didn't.

There is a regular column in our local newspaper that features a local teenager. The teen is asked the name of his or her best friend and the answer is always the same—"my parents."

It took thirty years for my parents to become my friends. Before that, we were enemy combatants, locked in a mortal struggle for superiority.

I've been wondering when it was adults went from being children's enemies to their best friends. I was talking with my neighbor Jim about this one day when we were splitting firewood. Jim is a seat-of-the-pants philosopher, not big on books, but strong on conventional wisdom.

"How come our children like us?" I asked. "Whatever happened to the good old days when children despised adults?"

Jim picked up an ax. He always thinks better with a tool in his hand. "Folks move too much," he said. "Used to be, folks stayed put. Kids made kid friends and the grown-ups made grown-up friends. Now we're moving around too much, and the whole natural order of things is upset."

"Did you have any adult friends when you were a kid?" I asked.

"Nope."

"Did the parents of other children feel free to yell at you?"

"Yep."

"I miss those days."

One of the sadder trends of modern life is asking someone where they grew up and hearing them reply, "All over." It used to be when someone was from all over, their father was in the military or ministry. But today, companies move their employees from one state to another, pieces in a corporate chess game. Everyone's on the move, trading one beige house for another every few years. When we bought our home, it was painted red. The realtor suggested we paint it a neutral color so it would be easier to sell when we moved. We hadn't even moved in and were already being told how to sell the place. I don't know of any other culture that would tolerate the disruption of constantly being moved, the ripping out of our roots, but we Americans accept it as part and parcel of modern life.

I've lived in the same small town a good chunk of my life and finally know my way around. If the people at my job told me I had to move, I'd find a new job. I don't have the energy to learn the peculiarities of a new place. When there's a heavy snow and the cars can't make it up the hill in front of the park, I know to take the back way home. When the storm drain in front of my house clogs, I know to call Rob Roberts, who'll send a man to clean it out. Janet at the library knows what kind of books I like and sets them aside for me to read. Leonard at the Co-op knows I enjoy sweet corn and leaves a grocery sack full on my back porch each August. Larry at the Marathon station knows when my cars need to be serviced, comes and gets them, then lets me pay the next time I'm in for gas. Kim, who cuts my hair, knows where my cowlick is and how to keep it from sticking up. Brigette at the pizza place knows I don't like mushrooms and prefer my salad dressing on the side. Joe the chimney sweep knows to clean our flue every October, and Sandy knows to bring me nine ricks of oak wood each April.

It's taken me years to arrange my life so conveniently. If I were to move, I'd have to start all over.

But after talking with my neighbor Jim, it occurs to me that the chief benefit of staying put is the sense of shared duty. My neighbors are beginning to feel free to yell at my children, and I'm starting to yell at theirs. It's feeling more like my childhood all the time.

We can pass all the laws we want, reform our schools, lobby our politicians, write our blogs, and take out ads, but my nickel is on the folks who meddle in the lives of children, those benevolent dictators who care less about being a child's friend and more about what kind of people we'll one day turn loose in the world.

These are the reasons I stay where I do—that I mind my business and everyone else's, and they know and mind mine. Some people don't like small towns, finding the scrutiny unbearable, but I prefer to think of it as the tie that binds.

A Growing Problem

My wife is not a heavy person, though she is plagued with insecurities about her weight. When we first married, we purchased a set of bathroom scales. We didn't have much money, and the scales were poorly made. The first time Joan stood on them, the needle broke free and made a run for it, looping the dial several times before stopping at three hundred and twenty pounds. After I revived her, I pointed out that the scales were broken, but she's been jumpy around scales ever since.

When I married Joan, she was tall and slender and still is. I, however, have gained forty pounds and now weigh a hundred and sixty. That might not seem excessive, but you should bear in mind I'm only four feet tall. People who've known me a long time say I look better with the extra weight. I was so skinny as a child I could reach my hand inside a milk bottle and pull out a hard-boiled egg.

When I turned forty, I began to notice the waist-bands on my pants were growing tighter. I asked Joan not to dry them so long, but she didn't heed my advice, and they kept shrinking. Around the same time, the neckbands on my shirts no longer fit. I then reached the only reasonable conclusion I could—someone had snuck into my home and altered my clothes.

I was discussing this bizarre incident at Frank's Restaurant one day at lunchtime. I stopped in for my usual plate of lasagna, garlic bread, and soda pop, and Bill Eddy happened to be there. I could tell his pants and shirt had been altered too. We chatted over a piece of Frank's homemade three-layer chocolate cake, speculating on who might be behind this nefarious deed, but arrived at no conclusion. Ours is a town of practical jokers, the possible culprits too numerous to contemplate.

I mulled over this mystery that night, sitting in my recliner. My wife wanted me to go for a walk with her, but I was too busy thinking. It was a good thing, because my blood-sugar level dropped and I had to eat a candy bar and drink a Coke. I felt a lot better after that and was able to take a nap.

The next day, I went to visit Leon Martin. He and his wife, Joan, own the Dairy Queen in town. I make it a point to visit them each day the Dairy Queen is open. Leon knows I have a discriminating palate and asked if I wanted to try the new coconut-cream-pie–flavored Blizzard, so I ate one as a favor to him. I told him it was quite tasty, but I could tell he thought I was saying that just to make him feel good, so I ate another one to demonstrate my sincerity.

I asked him how long his wife dried his clothes.

"Too long," he said. "My clothes are always shrinking."

It appeared this was a growing problem.

I got back in my car and drove a block to the library, where I visited with Janet, the librarian. The library was celebrating Literacy Month, and Janet informed me I had read enough books that month to qualify for a prize—three candy bars. There are four people in my family, and I knew if I took home only three candy bars, someone would feel left out, so I went ahead and ate them there, rather than hurt someone's feelings.

When I got back in my truck, I noticed it was overdue for an oil change, so I drove it down the hill to Larry's gas station. I have been after him for some time to stock Cokes in the little glass bottles, but he's always resisted. "Try one of these," he said, handing me a Yoo-hoo.

I was thirsty after eating three candy bars, so I went ahead and drank it. It wasn't bad, but it wasn't Coke.

Larry is very trim. His clothes appear to fit perfectly. "Who does your laundry?" I asked.

"My wife."

"Tell her she does a nice job."

I told him how my wife was always overdrying my clothes, causing them to shrink.

As long as I was there, I decided to have Larry adjust the brakes, so I drank another Yoo-hoo while I waited. They were starting to grow on me.

When I got home, my family asked me to join them on a bicycle ride, but I had work to do. The grass needed cutting, so I begged off the bicycle ride. I mow with a riding mower, which isn't as easy as it looks. It involves a lot of shifting, and if you're not careful, you could easily throw out a shoulder or wreck an elbow.

After all that work, I was famished. Joan wasn't home yet, so I had a Hostess cupcake to tide me over. Have you ever noticed how those have gone up in price while getting smaller? One cupcake used to be enough to fill me up, but now it takes two and sometimes three. Fortunately, after Joan came home, she cooked hamburgers on the grill. My oldest son doesn't care for hamburgers, so I ate his too. I didn't want to, but I hate to see food go to waste.

It had been a productive day, and my stamina was fading. So after supper I decided to relax in my recliner. *Seinfeld* was on, so I took our television out of the closet and watched it. Then I read a book until it was almost bedtime. I don't sleep well on an empty stomach, so Joan fixed me a bowl of ice cream.

When I went upstairs, I couldn't find my pajamas. I asked my wife if she knew where they were. "In the dryer," she said. "I washed them today."

The dryer is in the basement, and my shoulder was starting to hurt from all the mowing, so Joan got them for me. But she'd obviously left them in there too long. Now they've shrunk even more, and I have to get a new pair of pajamas. I love my wife, but her continued refusal to accept responsibility is starting to annoy me.

Things I Ponder While Sitting in Meeting

Nearly every Sunday morning, we have visitors to our Quaker meeting for worship. They enter the front door tentatively, peering around the 1892 meetinghouse, taking in the oaken pews, the fine cracks in the horsehair plaster, the carved pulpit that rests on a six-inch plywood base, raised when Gene Lewis, six foot four, was our pastor in 1957. The pulpit had been made in the early 1900s under the ecclesial leadership of Sarah Woodard, five foot two.

A Regulator clock hangs next to the door. Dick Givan winds it each Sunday morning. Dick was, for many years, the chief justice of the Supreme Court of Indiana, but now is our resident clock winder, dish washer, and snow shoveler. Since Quakers are wary of honorifics and titles, believing they confer a privileged status, Dick keeps it simple. "Call me Dick," he says, greeting our visitors.

I watch the visitors during the silence. When we fall quiet, they look around, thinking someone has forgotten to speak. They are embarrassed for the poor soul. This typifies the general lack of awareness about Quakers, which is our fault. We are evangelically bashful and too thrifty to advertise. Consequently, ignorance about us abounds. The customary response when someone discovers I'm a Quaker is either "I thought you all were dead," "Aren't you like the Amish?" or "The oatmeal people, right?"

Though the Bible warns against pride, we Quakers take a certain pleasure in our eccentricities. Anyone can be a Baptist, but it takes real character to be a Quaker. We don't vote on church matters and mistrust would-be bishops. When we don't agree on a matter, we talk about it, sometimes for years. Every now and then, a Quaker might overestimate his or her importance and grow officious, but he or she is politely ignored. When an unsuitable person is nominated to a position of spiritual leadership, a Quaker never says, "You've got to be kidding." We might want to, but we never would. Instead, we smile and say, "That name would not have occurred to me." That is hardball, Quaker-style.

There is too much hardball in religion today—too much invective and taking no prisoners—much of it piped through the air and into our homes, telling us whom to hate and what to fear. The Quakers in my meeting joke about striking back, of televising our meeting for worship. One hundred and twenty Quakers sitting on oaken pews in an 1892 meetinghouse. A little singing, a dab of preaching, then thirty minutes of silence. Viewers jabbing at the volume button on their remotes, then whacking their televisions thinking they've gone on the blink, their anger mounting.

I'm not sure whether our visitors are put off by our low-church simplicity or charmed by it, but I can usually tell who will come back for another visit. Men wearing ties seldom return. I'm among the few men in my meeting who wear a tie, mostly to keep my congregation off balance. I sit on the liberal side of religion, at God's left hand, but dress conservatively and am hard to pin down.

People carrying big Bibles usually don't come back. We have perfectly serviceable Bibles in our pews and see no need to arm ourselves with additional copies. This strikes some visitors as theologically suspect, that we're not sufficiently biblical. One Sunday, a man visited carrying a Bible so large it needed built-in wheels. He didn't make it halfway through meeting for worship.

I'm embarrassed to admit it, but when I saw him, I was reminded of Little Red Riding Hood and the wolf. "My, what a big Bible you have," said Little Red. "All the better to bludgeon you," answered the wolf.

Men who are handy with tools think twice about returning. They spend the hour studying our old meetinghouse, envisioning a lifetime of indentured servitude stretching before them. We reel them in slowly, first asking them to replace a fuse. When they agree, the hook is set. Within the year, we'll have them balancing precariously on ladders, painting soffits, and reroofing the meetinghouse. If they should fall from the ladder and perish, we Quakers do a wonderful job with memorial services.

If you are fortunate enough to expire in the bosom of a Quaker meeting, you will receive a send-off like no other. Dozens of people will testify to your fine qualities, whether you had any or not. We'll bear your casket out the meetinghouse door, down the stairs, and across the road to the cemetery, where you'll be lowered carefully in the ground. Then your loved ones will gather in the meetinghouse dining room and partake of meat loaf, green beans, orange Jell-O with carrot slivers, iced tea, and a variety of homemade pies. I once conducted a funeral service and had thirteen members of the deceased's family join our meeting the next week.

In the twenty-first century, this is what it means to be Quaker in my neck of the woods—retaining some traditions, while jettisoning others. It remains to be seen whether we have distinguished correctly between the essential and the trivial. I ponder these matters and more while sitting in meeting, the Regulator clock subtracting the minutes until we shall meet the Lord.

Contentment

"My greatest blessing," my mother-in-law, Ruby Apple, tells me, "is that I have always been content."

She tells me this often, so I know it must be true. She never says, "My greatest blessing is that I have enjoyed good health," or "My greatest blessing is that I married well." Though she appreciates her good health and marriage, she is most grateful for contentment, knowing it's a rarer bird.

It's tempting to think there's a correlation between material abundance, ease of life, and contentment, but that's not the case with Ruby. She was born into a poor family and moved from home at the age of fifteen to work as a housekeeper and attend high school. She's lived in the same small house since 1941, raised five children, worked alongside her husband on a patch of

Indiana ground, was widowed while the children were still home, and describes her life with words like "fortunate" and "happy."

Where I see hardship, difficulty, and suffering, she sees strokes of good luck and blessing. If I didn't know her better, I'd think she wasn't right in the head, but she's saner than anyone I've ever met.

I've known Ruby twenty-five years. Once, during the early years of our association, I was seated at her kitchen table. Ruby was washing dishes, and I was reading a magazine article about happiness. It contained a quiz readers could take to gauge their well-being. I decided to test Ruby, so read her the questions, and marked her responses. According to the quiz, she was supposed to be miserable. The man who wrote the quiz was a doctor of psychology, so I know he must be right. I keep expecting Ruby to face reality and be depressed, but she stubbornly insists on being cheerful.

I'm not the jealous type, but I envy Ruby her contentment. I'm always aiming for some elusive happiness and missing. Like most Americans, I'm guilty of thinking more stuff will make me happy, so I'm a vigorous gatherer of things that give me pleasure—chairs, books, and pocketknives. I'm most content when I'm sitting in a chair, reading a book, with a knife in my pocket. But the pleasure is fleeting. As soon as I get out of my chair, I'm prone to discontent.

Every month or so, I drive the hundred miles south to Ruby's home and take her to lunch. She lives in a remote part of the state where the local restaurants are unremarkable, but to Ruby it's all white tablecloths, silver, and crystal.

She orders the same thing no matter where we go—a chicken sandwich and "a clear soda." In all the years we've done this, she's never been displeased.

"How's your sandwich, Ruby?"

"Delicious."

On our way home, she talks about the sandwich and recounts her long history with chickens. "We'd get two hundred baby chickens at Corydon every spring. Then along about September, we'd butcher most of them. Kept some of them back for laying hens, but we ate most of them. Howard, he'd work the chopping block, and me and the girls dipped 'em in the kettle, then plucked 'em."

It seems rather grisly to me, a fowlish holocaust, but Ruby smiles at the memory; her countenance is one of pure pleasure.

"Yes," she says, on our ride home, "chickens have been awful good to me."

I once asked Ruby the secret of her contentment, and she looked at me, thoroughly mystified. Secret? What secret? She smiled and went on about her day.

Why are folks who think the least about contentment the most content?

I suspect Ruby's "secret" is low expectations. She grew up in hardship, assumed most of her life would follow that pattern, and so was surprised and grateful when good came her way. Too many of us approach life in the opposite manner. We believe the world owes us a great deal, are disappointed when it fails to deliver, and think ourselves deprived. If life were mashed potatoes, we'd see the lumps and Ruby would see the gravy.

Perhaps our headlong pursuit of happiness is the enemy. Since Ruby never believed the world owed her happiness, she's found it in small ways, in the slightest things, cultivating the wise habit of seeing the silver lining and not the cloud.

This is a great irony—people who have every reason to be content seldom are. Though happiness is their aim, it seems always out of reach. I wonder if gratefulness is the bridge from sorrow to joy, spanning the chasm of our anxious striving. Freed from the burden of unbridled desires, we can enjoy what we have, celebrate what we've attained, and appreciate the familiar. For if we can't be happy *now*, we'll likely not be happy *when*.

Camping

When I was a child, it was my custom to regularly retire to the woods, bearing a knapsack with a rolled sleeping bag tied to it with shoelaces. My pack held a small frying pan, a spoon, an assortment of canned goods, a canteen of water, a hatchet, a box of Ohio Blue Tip matches, and a sheet of plastic in the event of rain. I passed many leisurely days and nights in the woods surrounding our town, accompanied by two or three friends, all of whom were similarly equipped. I started doing this when I was twelve years old, in all types of weather, and never once returned home in worse condition than when I had left.

Whenever I speak of those days, people say, "Well, you wouldn't let a child do that today." But I would let my sons do it in a moment. Those evenings spent beside the campfire, in the woods outside our town, remain the source of my most pleasant childhood memories. I return to them happily and often, and would be delighted if, in their later years, my sons could enjoy similar recollections.

The marvel of camping was, and continues to be, its simplicity. By camping, I'm not referring to that wheeled wonder, the recreational vehicle. We've not yet coined an appropriate verb to describe staying in an RV, but it isn't "camping." My publisher once rented a motor home and sent my family and me through the South on a book tour. Each night, we would pull into a paved lot, tether the vehicle to life support, enjoy a delicious meal, then sleep in air-conditioned comfort. The experience was quite enjoyable, but it wasn't camping. A general rule of thumb is this: If you return home smelling clean, if your clothing is fresh and pressed, your hair washed and combed, you haven't been camping.

Each August, my neighbor Jim and his sons drive to Canada, canoe the Boundary Waters, sleep on boulders, get bit by mosquitoes as big as pigeons, and come home exhausted, swollen with disease, and stinking to high heaven. By golly, that is camping! As they age, Jim's sons whine about having to go, but he brooks no dissent. It is part of his plan to have his children leave home at the age of eighteen and become hardworking,

God-fearing, taxpaying, homeowning, debt-burdened Americans like the rest of us.

My finest camping memory happened when I was fifteen and went to McCormick's Creek State Park with David Runyon and Bill Eddy for an entire week. Bill's father drove us the fifty miles to the park, deposited us at the entrance, and then left before discovering one member of the camping party had to be eighteen, which we weren't. David Runyon raised his hand, solemnly swore he was nineteen, and we were admitted.

We camped in a huge tent David had unearthed from his basement. Once erected, it appeared the circus had come to town. The first night, Bill Eddy threw an opened can of mixed vegetables at me. I ducked, and they splattered against the tent ceiling, where they stuck. During our week's stay, lima beans and carrot slices would drop from the ceiling onto us while we slept, a light sprinkle of vegetables.

If I could regain any week of my life, it would be that one. I hold it now in the vivid colors of memory, like the lush hues of a Technicolor movie. Though I had been away from home, never had I ventured such a distance for such a duration. No parents hovered over us, urging us to change our underwear and eat our vegetables. We were blessedly free and took full advantage of our liberation. Though we are now adults and free to do whatever we wish, the rules of propriety keep us from it.

The treasure of that free week was not just the liberty, but our ignorance of decorum. We sinned boldly and felt no shame. Every boy should enjoy such a week.

I met my first love there, a redhead from Ohio. My infatuation required no work on her part. Indeed, she appeared not even to know I existed. I never spoke a word to her, but watched her from afar, my heart thumping, my palms sweating, and liked to imagine she felt the same way toward me, even though I had dried lima beans stuck to my hair.

Liberty has its advantages, but on that trip I learned the danger of freedom unchecked by law. I had taken along two prized objects—a pocket watch and pocket-knife—which I left behind one afternoon on my sleeping bag in the tent. I returned to find them missing. When I told my father, who'd assured me campers were reverent, honest, and helpful, he was skeptical.

"Must have been a raccoon," my father said. "They like shiny things."

If so, it was an incredibly agile raccoon, able to unzip our tent, filch my goods, then thoughtfully zip the tent shut on its way out.

The last night of our trip, a storm rose up and pounded us.

"I wonder if it's true," Bill Eddy asked, midway through the storm, "that if you touch a tent while it's raining, it will leak."

It is, and it did. The night passed with rain trickling upon us, the tent swaying back and forth to the mad beat of thunder. We debated whether to seek shelter in the outhouse, but the prospect of sniffing the fumes of our past was more than we could bear, so we stayed put, curled in soggy heaps on the tent floor.

With no stout walls to shed the storm, there was a slender distance between well-being and hazard. In one long night, we learned human frailty, the myth of safety, and the limits of teenage bravado. We finished the week more reverent and subdued.

In my trove of camping supplies, I treasure most a red Coleman lantern I inherited from my grandfather. It is in fine working order, and whenever a storm slams in from the west, knocking out our power, I retrieve the lantern from our basement, place it on our kitchen table, open a window, and light it. It casts a benevolent glow across the room, carving a nook of light while the heavens flash and boom.

I sit in the kitchen, worried the basement might fill with water, while my boys run about, skittish with excitement. Watching them, I am once again a child, deep in the dark woods, feeling the delicious swirl of danger, recalling my small victories over fear and the splendid joy of dawn.

On the Road Again

When I was in Mr. Evanoff's fifth-grade class we studied the great explorers—Columbus, Magellan, Marco Polo, Ponce de Leon, and Bob Pearcy. Bob Pearcy is from our town. He and his wife, Marthalyn, traveled across America in their RV. They had a map of the United States affixed to the rear of their Fleetwood, where they posted state stickers of various colors, revealing their westward expansion. Some famous explorers put on airs, but not the Pearcys. They still attend the First Christian Church, where Marthalyn helps with Sunday school and Bob serves as a deacon. As far as I can tell, fame hasn't gone to their heads one bit.

I have long admired the Pearcys' savoir-faire, the breadth of their knowledge and experience, their ability to be at home wherever they are. The world is the palette from which their lives are painted.

When Bob wasn't on the road, he was the publisher of the *Danville Gazette,* a Democratic newspaper in a town of red-hot Republicans. From an early age, I've been drawn to seditious literature and used to read the *Gazette* under my covers at night using a flashlight. One night, my father caught me. "What's that you're reading?" he asked.

"A *Playboy,*" I answered, thinking quickly.

"That better be a *Playboy.* If I find out you've been reading the *Gazette,* you'll be in trouble."

Sometimes I think Bob left town for the rest.

I hail from more settled stock. It took our branch of the Gulleys two hundred years to make it from North Carolina to Indiana, and that pretty well soured us on travel. When I was growing up, my family's idea of exotic travel was to drive the back roads to Cooper's Hardware in Stilesville to buy our Christmas tree. It was only twelve miles, but my father would return home spent, a shell of his former self.

My wife grew up on a dairy farm where the cows needed to be milked twice a day, so her family never went anywhere either. She met me on her first long trip away from home, which has given her pause about travel ever since.

I became a writer hoping it would spare me the miseries of the commute, but soon learned travel was part and parcel of the experience. The deepest loneliness was at night, driving past people's homes in some distant city, glimpsing their shadowed movements. I would think of my family and wonder what they were doing at that precise moment. Sam would be sitting in the chair next to the woodstove in our kitchen, reading, I imagined. Spencer would be stretched out across the floor, nuzzling Zipper, our dog. Joan would be at the kitchen table, working that day's crossword puzzle. I would mentally insert myself in that agreeable scene, seated beside my wife, lending a hand with the puzzle. Native Americans, I've been told, limited their travel each day to permit their souls to catch up with their bodies. That was the problem with me. While my body was in Birmingham, my spirit was back home.

I once knew a beautiful soul named Fern Hadley, who died while on a trip to Portugal. At her Quaker memorial service, her son-in-law rose from his pew and said, "Wherever Fern was, she made her home."

His words summarized beautifully what I so cherished about Fern—not just her ability to be at home, but to make others around her feel at home, feel a part of things.

I wish I had that gift—to see the world as my home, and not just this little corner of it. I'm working on it, but progress is slow. When I'm on the road, I find myself yearning for the familiar, lamenting where I am, wishing I were elsewhere, namely, home. What a waste of the present that is.

"This world is not my home," the old hymn goes. But the song is wrong. It is my home, all of it, everywhere, and yours too. And the sooner we realize that, the better our world will be.

Spring and All It Portends

Each October, my wife buys a new calendar for the approaching year. Depending on her mood, it will feature scenery from around the country—New England's covered bridges, California redwoods, Spanish moss. Or it will be austere—no art, no embellishment of any sort, just days and weeks and months. One year though, she attended a fall festival and was given a calendar by an ambitious nun hoping to lure us toward Catholicism by means of a refrigerator calendar.

There was scarcely any room on the calendar for me to write my own obligations, for all the Holy Days of Obligation the Catholics had printed on it. It seemed to me an ominous foreshadowing—were I to join up with the Catholics, I would have no time for my plans because of their plans for me.

But no matter the calendar, ecclesial or otherwise, I always turn to March to see when the first day of spring will fall and circle it in red, though I have noticed spring pays little attention to the manufacturers of calendars. She strolls into town when she's ready and not a moment sooner.

I've had a long and torrid love affair with spring. My most glowing memories are associated with that season and its arrival. It was a high moment when our junior high school principal, Mr. Peters, would come on the intercom and announce that we were free to go outside and sit on the lawn during our lunch hour. This usually occurred on an early April day, when the sun was full, the mercury pushing just above sixty, and the daffodils showing their green tips. Now, thirty years later, Mr. Peters's son is the principal and the children still assemble on the lawn every spring. If that custom ever ends, I'm not sure how we would know it was spring.

In the days before radial tires, spring's arrival could also be gauged by the number of anxious old men gathered at Logan's Mobil. I would overhear their worried conversations every morning, on my way to school, when I would stop in for my daily libation of Nehi and peanuts.

They would be gathered near the cash register, speculating on the weather. This was back in the days when the prudent man arranged for Wally to mount his snow tires the week after Thanksgiving and remove them when the threat of snow had safely passed. When that day was, was subject to vigorous debate. There were always several men arguing for restraint, men with long memories, warning that winter hadn't had her final say. They recalled spring storms from their childhood dumping great heaps of snow on a town that had cast off its winter garb. The latest date for measurable snowfall was May 8, 1923, but to these anxious souls it was yesterday; the memory is still fresh, their joints still achy with cold.

I face the same quandary every spring. There is a shelf in my garage that, in the winter, holds my lawn edger and, in the summer, my snowblower. Each spring, I spend a few uneasy weeks worrying whether I have switched them out too hastily. Logan's is now closed, the sages have moved to the Senior Center, which I don't inhabit, so there is no one to counsel me on such matters. I need an old man in my neighborhood who will stop past my garage each week to tell me my business.

I have lately been thinking about the rashness of youth—those straining, exuberant colts frolicking on the school lawn—and the timidity of the aged—those gas-station prophets who preach caution and restraint. It seems to me a backward equation. One would think that inexperience and immaturity would cause us to hang back, maybe dip our toe in the water before plunging in; and, conversely, that knowledge and expertise would embolden us, make us more daring and willing to risk. It doesn't speak well of the world we've created that life makes us more leery, more guarded, more vigilant and timid.

I was speaking with a Mormon friend not long ago and asked him why they sent out their nineteen-year-olds to talk about faith and life. My words were something to this effect: "What do nineteen-year-olds know about life?"

He laughed and agreed, then said they sent out the young people because the older people, who did know something about life, wouldn't go. That, in a nutshell, is our problem—people who don't know much are telling the rest of us what to do, while the wise and experienced are staying home.

When I think of the mentors I've had, it occurs to me how seamlessly they joined the eagerness of youth with the prudence of age. Their energy was well channeled, their enthusiasm artfully directed by their wisdom. They never hesitated to frolic, but were careful not to twist an ankle.

This is spring, and wisdom, to me—new life dancing, leaping here, twirling there, casting off the winter garb, but keeping fresh the memory of cold, knowing the bloom is frail and the months roll blithely on.

My History with Easter

Some days loom large in memory, and an Easter from my childhood is one of them. It had been our custom to celebrate Easter at St. Mary's Catholic Church, but I recall one Easter, when I was about seven, that we threw off tradition and went out of town for our religion, a hundred miles south to my grandparents' home in Vincennes. I suppose I remember it for two reasons—the change in location and my father's presence.

We drove down on Saturday and were dispersed among various kinfolk, then collected again the next morning and walked the four blocks to the Old Cathedral, the adults stepping carefully along the root-heaved sections of sidewalk, rent like the temple curtain, and we children roaming ahead of them, scouting for Easter eggs.

I was never a big fan of church in my childhood, but that Easter holds a pleasant association for me—the white and golden finery, the thundering music, sitting next to my father, inhaling his Old Spice aftershave, every now and then sneaking a jelly bean from my suit pocket, raising my hands to my face in a posture of prayer, slipping the jelly bean into my mouth and sucking it down to a soft lump.

A deep gladness and lightness of heart accompanied the day. The winter concluded, the slush melted, the salt-rimmed streets scoured clean by the spring rains, the daffodils blossomed, and the hours of sunlight stretched on both ends of the day. When the priest stood and read from the book of Revelation, how Christ made all things new, nature nodded its agreement.

Easter would not work in any other season but spring. For all we know, Jesus could have resurrected in October, but it was a stroke of genius to celebrate his revival in spring, when renewal is more believable.

Every Easter, our Quaker meeting holds two worship services. This distresses my sons to no end, and they threaten a boycott. One worship service is tolerable, but having to sit through meeting twice in one morning seems unusually cruel. Although my boys wail at the prospect of church overload, I think they secretly delight in Easter, though they would deny this in the strongest language. We Quakers don't believe one day is more holy than another, but we left the door open and glitz and glamour slipped in. Even Bobby Heald, who ordinarily wears a motorcycle jacket, dons a sport coat and tie.

But not everyone welcomes the hoopla. I once spoke with a group of pastors and asked them their favorite Sunday. Easter came in last. Their complaints were as follows: noisy people, ambitious music sung by over-reaching soloists, funny hats, general chaos, and trying to remember the names of once-a-year visitors. As a fan of occasional mayhem, I enjoy Easter for those very reasons. For fifty-one weeks a year, we're sober and dignified. If folks want to hoot and wail and kick up their heels one Sunday a year, that's fine with me.

I used to expend much effort on my Easter sermons, twenty hours or more. It finally dawned on me that I could stand at the pulpit, read from the Betty Crocker cookbook, and people would still clap me on the back and say, "Good sermon, pastor. It really made me think." So now I put on my suit, weave together a string of clichés, and ask Mildred to crank up the volume on the organ when we sing "Christ the Lord Has Risen Today," and everyone goes home happy and glad to be alive.

But in any crowd there is a malcontent or two, and the Easter crowd is no exception. Someone invariably demands I speak out against the Easter Bunny. I am captivated by a great number of subjects, but have never worked up the enthusiasm to preach against rabbits, real or mythic. These are the same people who complain about Santa at Christmas and want me to take a swipe at Halloween. They're not happy unless someone somewhere is being censured.

People who track such things tell us that, next to Christmas, folks spend more money on Easter than any other holiday. I once received a phone call from a publisher asking if I would write an Easter book. He assured me I could "capture the Easter market." I never knew such a thing as the Easter market existed and have no interest in capturing it. These people are no different from the Easter Bunny haters. They both have an agenda, either one of which would spell the ruination of an otherwise fine holiday.

The Easter spirit is hard enough to sustain without bunny bashers and marketers trying to cut it off at the knees. Time also erodes its charm. My sons are now too old to believe in the Easter Bunny, but too young to provide me with grandchildren who would welcome that kindly rabbit. There ought to be a way a person could rent some five-year-olds for the day. Easter without a kid is like Christmas without a tree.

I tend to be optimistic, but a few things discourage me. Knowing my best Easters are likely behind me is one of them. But every now and then that sepia splendor shines through the haze, usually the night before, when we dip eggs at the kitchen table, the heady scent of vinegar rising from the rainbow cups. The smell brings back the mystery and wonder of Easters past. I'm seven years old and lapping my grandparents' backyard, clutching a grocery sack from the Buy-Rite, plucking violet eggs from tufts of still-brown grass. Seeking the new among the old, beside myself with the excitement of it.

The End Times

When I was young my family moved in a few doors down from Baker's Funeral Home. I learned to ride bikes and roller-skate in its parking lot. My older siblings and their belongings were conveyed to college in a hearse bearing the name Baker's Funeral Home on the side. I come from a family well served by the funeral industry.

Given that, it's not surprising that when I left home, I rented an apartment from a mortician, next door to a funeral parlor. I was asked to sign a contract vowing to conduct myself in a manner befitting the solemnity of death—no parties, no working on my car in the street, no loud music, no drinking or smoking or cursing. By then I was a Quaker and a model of rectitude, so I signed the contract and lived there a happy, but quiet, seven years.

The mortician, Norwood, was advanced in years and occasionally required my assistance retrieving a citizen whose earthly journey had concluded. I would don a white shirt, knot a tie around my neck, feeling the clench of death as I pulled it tight, slip on my dress pants and shoes, then ride with Norwood in the hearse to the nursing home, hospital, or farm field, wherever the dead had fallen. For my effort, twenty-five dollars was deducted from my rent. Some months, when money was scarce, I would pray for someone to succumb, a person for whom death would be sweet release, someone old and sick who wanted to die anyway.

Some of my most pleasant memories are associated with Norwood's funeral home. In fact, I met my wife there, when I peered out my kitchen window one summer evening, saw her walking past, and hurried outside to introduce myself. Two years later, we were married. To this day, whenever I drive by a funeral home, my heart beats a little faster and I break out in a sweat. Some people see funeral homes and are filled with foreboding. I see one and think of romance.

Though I don't think they've spawned any marriages, there are two funeral homes in my town, Weaver-Randolph and Baker's. The Bakers also owned the hardware store, which is how my family got their start with them. It was a stroke of marketing genius on the Bakers' part, to get people accustomed to doing business with them, selling them nuts, bolts, and nails over the years, forming a habit of commerce, so that when an undertaker was needed, Baker's naturally came to mind. Ten-penny nails and a toilet plunger one week, an oak coffin and burial vault the next.

Roughly half the families in our town are Baker families, the other half Weaver-Randolph families. In some towns, one's funeral home allegiance is determined by one's religion, but that isn't the case here. It appears the loyalties were determined long ago, by unknown and unspoken criteria, and we who've inherited that choice have little say in the matter. It is like being born with brown hair. You are either a Baker family or a Weaver-Randolph family, and there is little one can do about it. Every now and then, I overhear disgruntled locals vow to forsake one funeral home for another, but when their time draws near, they return to their former alliance like dying salmon revisiting the streams of their birth.

For years, both funeral homes sponsored Little League teams. I was on Baker's. Wearing a baseball uniform with the name of a funeral home on the shirt had a stultifying effect, and we lost nearly every game. Buck Leath was our coach and a fine man, but the sting of humiliation caused him to shun all things

Baker. When he passed away decades later, I conducted his funeral at Weaver-Randolph.

In our town, funerals are as much a social event as anything. Among our citizens are a number of professional mourners who flock to funerals like birds to a feeder. The slightest tie with the deceased can induce them to grieve. The newly departed have let down their guard, discretion falls by the wayside, and long-held secrets are ripe for the plucking. The professionals linger near the family, hoping a crumb of rumor might fall to the floor, a tiny indiscretion they may feast on for days.

But mine is not the only town captivated by death. In my wife's hometown, the local radio station announces the community death toll each morning at ten. The locals pause from their endeavors, turn up the volume, and listen closely to hear who has fallen to the Reaper's scythe. The hospital report follows, naming each patient, the malady, and the prospects. The townspeople track their neighbor's revival or decline, whichever the case may be, until the person can leave the hospital under his or her own power or be carried out by Harvey from McAdam's Mortuary.

Some people would like this ghoulish custom to end, but I support it. Dying is something we used to do at home, in the company of our family, friends, and pastor. Now it's done in hospital rooms or nursing homes, in between nursing shifts. If we're fortunate, an under-paid aide might be present to watch the red line of the heart monitor go flat, but for too many people dying is a lonely venture.

Unaccustomed to the rituals of death, we seem to find death a more unsettling prospect than our ances-tors did, who, not too many generations ago, cleaned and dressed the dead, laid them out in the front room, wept over them, then hand-dug the grave under the tree in the back corner of the cemetery. We hire out all that now, and consequently seem to fear death and its trappings in a way our elders didn't.

I was visiting a widow in my meeting one Sunday afternoon. She pointed to a corner of her living room and said in a casual manner, "This used to be a bed-room. My husband was born right in that corner. And he died there too." She seemed perfectly content to live among all those ghosts, indeed, seemed to find it a soft comfort.

But others don't sit so loosely with death. Millions of American Christians labor under the curious convic-tion that they won't die, that Jesus will descend on the clouds one bright day and carry them to heaven. But I'm betting they'll get there the same way we always have, compliments of heart disease, cancer, or plain bad luck. I realize those are mundane deaths compared to the ones described in the book of Revelation—being slain by a rider on a pale horse or having your ticket punched by a Lamb with seven horns—but extraordinary claims require extraordinary proof, and I'm not persuaded.

A life insurance salesman once told me, using statistical probability, the details of my end times. According to the actuarial tables, I will die of heart disease in a nursing home on March 7, 2048, at the ripe, old age of eighty-seven. Unless, of course, I am done in by a seven-headed beast next Tuesday. If that happens, take me to Baker's.

A Note to the Reader

*P*orch Talk is my fourteenth book. In addition to writing, I also serve as the co-pastor of Fairfield Friends Meeting near Indianapolis. If you're ever in the area, stop by and visit. If you would like directions to our meetinghouse, or want to contact me electronically, feel free to e-mail me at info@philipgulleybooks.com.

If you're reading one of my books in your book club and would like me to phone in for a visit, write to info@ philipgulleybooks.com and we'll get the ball rolling.

If you would like to discuss the possibility of my speaking at your church or event, please contact Mr. David Leonards at ieb@prodigy.net or (317) 926-7566.

Thank you again for buying and reading my books. I derive much joy in writing them; it is my prayer that you find joy in reading them.

Take care.

Philip Gulley

HARPER LUXE

THE NEW LUXURY IN READING

We hope you enjoyed reading
our new, comfortable print size and found it
an experience you would like to repeat.

Well — you're in luck!

HarperLuxe offers the finest in fiction and
nonfiction books in this same larger print size and
paperback format. Light and easy to read, HarperLuxe
paperbacks are for book lovers who want to see
what they are reading without the strain.

For a full listing of titles and
new releases to come, please visit our website:

www.HarperLuxe.com

HARPER LUXE

SEEING IS BELIEVING!